LOVE Flying Geese

27 Modern Quilt Projects
from *Love Patchwork & Quilting*

stashBOOKS®

an imprint of C&T Publishing

Text, photography, and artwork copyright © 2019 by *Love Patchwork & Quilting*

Publisher: Amy Marson

Creative Director: Gailen Runge

Acquisitions Editor / Compiler: Roxane Cerda

Managing Editor: Liz Aneloski

Cover/Book Designer: April Mostek

Production Coordinator: Tim Manibusan

Production Editor: Jennifer Warren

Cover photography by *Love Patchwork & Quilting*

Photography by *Love Patchwork & Quilting*, unless otherwise noted

Published by Stash Books, an imprint of C&T Publishing, Inc., P.O. Box 1456, Lafayette, CA 94549

Library of Congress Cataloging-in-Publication Data

Title: Love flying geese : 27 modern quilt projects from Love patchwork & quilting / editors of Love patchwork & quilting.

Other titles: Love patchwork & quilting.

Description: Lafayette, CA : Stash Books, an imprint of C&T Publishing, Inc., [2019]

Identifiers: LCCN 2018059385 | ISBN 9781617458422 (soft cover)

Subjects: LCSH: Quilting--Patterns. | Patchwork--Patterns. | Flying geese quilts.

Classification: LCC TT835 .L73 2019 | DDC 746.46/041--dc23

LC record available at https://lccn.loc.gov/2018059385

Printed in the USA

10 9 8 7 6 5 4 3 2 1

contents

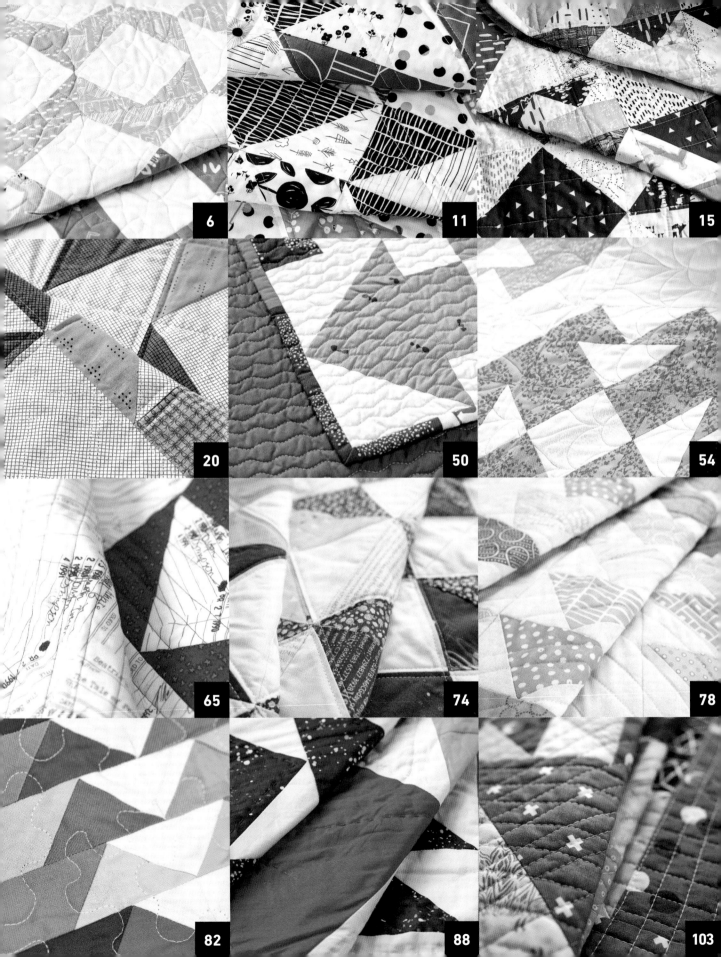

PASTEL TWIST

Peta Peace

Get clever with Flying Geese to combine pretty pastel points into a diamond design.

This quilt design really shows off how versatile the simple Flying Geese unit is!

COOL COLOURS
We love the mix of pastels and brights in this Pastel Thrift fabric collection from AGF.

QUILT

Finished quilt:
50in square approx

Fabrics used: Print fabrics are from the Pastel Thrift collection by AGF Studio for Art Gallery Fabrics.

You Will Need

Fabric A (pink print): ¾yd

Fabric B (grey print): ¾yd

Fabric C (yellow print): ¾yd

Fabric D (blue print): ¾yd

Background fabric (white): 2⅝yds

Backing fabric: 3¼yds

Batting: 56in square

Binding fabric: ½yd

NOTES

- Seam allowances are ¼in, unless otherwise noted.
- Wash and press all fabrics well before cutting.
- Press seams open, unless otherwise instructed.
- FG = Flying Geese
- RST = right sides together
- WOF = width of fabric
- Quilted by Diane's Quilting Quest

Cutting Out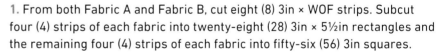

1. From both Fabric A and Fabric B, cut eight (8) 3in × WOF strips. Subcut four (4) strips of each fabric into twenty-eight (28) 3in × 5½in rectangles and the remaining four (4) strips of each fabric into fifty-six (56) 3in squares.

2. From both Fabric C and Fabric D, cut eight (8) 3in × WOF strips. Subcut four (4) strips of each fabric into twenty-two (22) 3in × 5½in rectangles and the remaining four (4) strips of each fabric into forty-four (44) 3in squares.

3. From the white background fabric cut thirty (30) 3in × WOF strips. Subcut fifteen (15) strips into one hundred (100) 3in × 5½in rectangles and fifteen (15) strips into two hundred (200) 3in squares.

4. From the binding fabric, cut six (6) 2¼in × WOF strips.

TOP TIP

When piecing the rows, press the seams in alternate directions—this will create nesting seams that will make piecing the quilt top a breeze.

Making the Blocks

5. Take one 3in × 5½in white rectangle and two 3in Fabric A squares. On the wrong side of each square mark a diagonal line from corner to corner.

6. With RST, place a square on one corner of the rectangle, with the diagonal line running from the bottom corner to the top edge. *Fig. A*

7. Stitch on the marked line and then trim ¼in beyond the stitched line. Flip the corner open and press the seam towards the triangle. Repeat for the other corner to make one Flying Geese unit. *Fig. B*

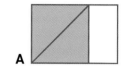

A

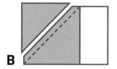  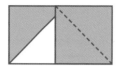  

B

8. Repeat Steps 5–7 with the remaining Fabric A 3in squares to make a total of twenty-eight FG units with Fabric A corners.

9. Repeat Steps 5–8 with the 3in × 5½in Fabric A rectangles and fifty-six of the 3in white squares to make a total of twenty-eight FG units with white corners. *Fig. C*

C

10. With the triangles pointing upwards, join a Fabric A corner FG unit to the top edge of a white corner FG unit. *Fig. D*

Repeat to make a total of twenty-eight double FG units.

11. Take two double FG units and join on the white FG unit edges, with the points of the double FG units pointing in opposite directions, to complete one block. *Fig. E*

Repeat to make a total of fourteen blocks, which should measure 5½in × 10½in.

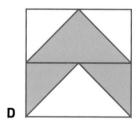

D

12. Repeat Steps 5–10 to make a total of fifty blocks as follows:

• Fourteen Fabric B/white blocks

• Eleven Fabric C/white blocks

• Eleven Fabric D/white blocks

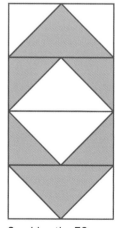

E

Combine the FG units to make the pointed blocks.

Think about your colours when laying out blocks to make the fabrics pop.

Diamond quilting echoes the diamond shape block design.

Orientate the blocks differently for an interesting design.

Experiment with different quilt top layouts to get your print placement just right.

Assembling the Quilt Top

13. Arrange the blocks into seven rows as shown, referring to the layout diagram for placement. From top to bottom, in rows one, four and seven, ten blocks are arranged vertically. In rows two, three, five and six, five blocks are arranged horizontally.

14. Join the blocks into rows, pressing the seams of alternate rows in opposite directions. Rows one, four and seven should measure 50½in × 10½in and rows two, three, five and six should measure 50½in × 5½in.

15. Join the rows to complete the quilt top, which should measure 50½in square.

Layout diagram

Quilting and Finishing

16. Cut the backing fabric in half across the width. Remove the selvedges and re-join the pieces along the length with a ½in seam. The backing needs to be least 2in–3in bigger all around than the quilt top.

17. Press the quilt top well. Make a quilt sandwich by placing the backing fabric right side down, the batting on top, then the quilt top centrally and right side up. The backing and batting are slightly larger than the quilt top. Baste the layers together.

18. Quilt as desired. This quilt was quilted with meandering diamond shapes.

19. Trim the excess batting and backing and square up the quilt.

20. Sew the binding strips together end-to-end using diagonal seams. Press the seams open and trim away the dog-ears. Fold in half lengthwise, WST, and press.

21. Sew the binding to the right side of the quilt, folding a mitre at each corner, then fold the binding over to the back of the quilt and hand stitch in place to finish.

LIGHT AND DARK
Jenn Nevitt

Mix bold monochrome shades with pale pastel tones to make simple FG units into a striking quilt design.

PERFECT MATCH
Pick your fave shade in the quilt and coordinate it with your bed linen.

QUILT

Finished quilt:
60in × 72in approx

Fabrics used: Print fabrics are from the Lagom collection by AGF Studio for Art Gallery Fabrics.

NOTES

- Seam allowances are ¼in, unless otherwise noted.
- FG = Flying Geese
- HST = half-square triangles
- RST = right sides together
- WOF = width of fabric
- WST = wrong sides together

Cutting Out

1. From the dark fabrics cut a total of twenty-three (23) 9¼in squares and forty-five (45) 5in squares.

2. From the light fabrics cut a total of ninety-two (92) 4⅞in squares and forty-five (45) 5in squares.

3. From the binding fabric cut eight (8) 2½in × WOF strips.

Colour pops of pink and blue brighten up monochrome prints.

Piecing the Flying Geese Units

4. Take four 4⅞in light squares. On the wrong side of each light square mark a diagonal line from corner to corner.

5. Take a one 9¼in dark square and place it right side up. RST, place a light square on two opposite corners, with the diagonal lines running from corner to corner of the dark square. The light squares will overlap. Sew ¼in each side of the marked line. *Fig. A*

6. Cut the squares apart on the marked line and press the units open. *Fig. B*

7. Take one of the units from Step 6 and, RST, place a light square on the remaining dark corner, with the marked line running from the dark corner to the middle. Sew ¼in each side of the marked line. *Fig. C*

8. Cut the units apart on the marked line. *Fig. D*

Press the units open to give two Flying Geese units. *Fig. E*

9. Repeat Steps 7 and 8 with the remaining unit from Step 6 and the remaining light square to make a total of four FG units. Trim each one to 8½in × 4½in.

10. Repeat Steps 4–9 to make a total of ninety-two FG units. You need ninety, so will have two left over.

Piecing the HST Units

11. Take one 5in dark square and one 5in light square. On the wrong side of the light square mark a diagonal line from corner to corner. Place the squares RST, with the marked square on top.

12. Stitch ¼in either side of the marked line and then cut through both layers on the marked line. *Fig. F*

13. Open the units out and press. Keeping the 45-degree line of your ruler aligned with the diagonal seam, trim to 4½in square. You will now have two HSTs. *Fig. G*

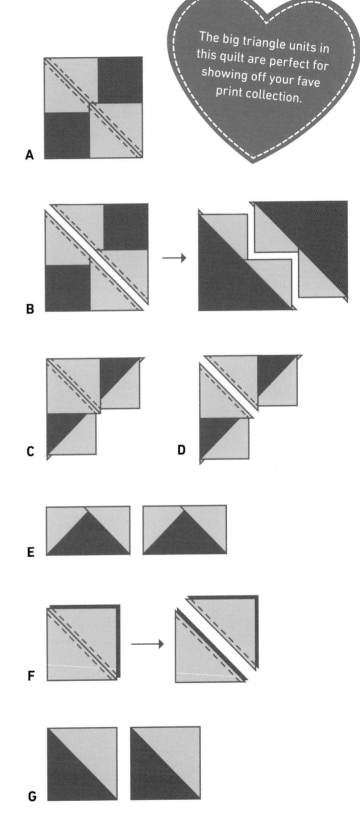

The big triangle units in this quilt are perfect for showing off your fave print collection.

A

B

C   D

E

F

G

Assembling the Quilt Top

14. Take three FG units and three HSTs. Arrange into three rows of one FG unit and one HST unit each as shown.

15. Sew the units into rows, then join the rows to make one block. *Fig. H*

16. Repeat Steps 14 and 15 to make a total of thirty blocks.

17. Arrange the blocks into six rows of five blocks each, referring to the photograph for placement.

18. Once you are happy with your block arrangement, sew them into rows, then join the rows to complete the quilt top.

Quilting and Finishing

19. Cut the backing fabric in half across the width. Remove the selvedges and re-join the pieces along the length with a ½in seam. Press the seam open.

20. Press the quilt top and backing well. Make a quilt sandwich by placing the backing fabric right side down, the batting on top, then the quilt top centrally and right side up. The backing and batting are slightly larger than the quilt top. Baste the layers together using your preferred method.

21. Quilt as desired. Jenn quilted pairs of diagonal lines approx ½in apart at 2¼in intervals across the quilt.

22. Trim off the excess batting and backing fabric and square up the quilt.

23. Join the binding strips together end-to-end using diagonal seams. Press the seams open and trim away the dog-ears. Fold in half lengthwise, WST, and press.

24. Sew the binding to the right side of the quilt, folding a mitre at each corner.

25. Fold the binding over to the back of the quilt and hand stitch in place to finish.

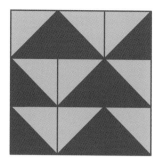

H

COLOUR STUDY 1
Karen Lewis

Experiment with tonal shades and print movement to turn simple blocks into a graphic diamond design.

PERFECT PAIR
Warm up cool greys with sunny springtime yellows and blues.

QUILT

Finished quilt:
44in × 64in approx

Fabrics used: Print fabrics are from the Observer collection by April Rhodes for Art Gallery Fabrics, along with solids from the Pure Elements Solids collection, also by Art Gallery Fabrics, that Karen screen-printed.

You Will Need

Print fabrics: 1½yds

Background fabrics: 2yds

Backing fabric: 2¾yds

Batting: 50in × 70in

Binding fabric: ½yd

NOTES

- Seam allowances are ¼in, unless otherwise noted.
- Press seams open unless otherwise instructed.
- FG = Flying Geese
- RST = right sides together
- WOF = width of fabric
- WST = wrong sides together

Cutting Out

1. From the print fabrics cut a total of sixteen (16) 9¼in squares and twelve (12) 5¼in squares.

2. From the background fabrics cut a total of:

- Sixty-four (64) 4⅞in squares
- Forty-eight (48) 2⅞in squares
- Forty-eight (48) 4½in × 2½in rectangles

3. From the binding fabric cut six (6) 2½in × WOF strips.

Textured fabric adds movement to the quilt top.

Making the FG Units

4. Take four 4⅞in background fabric squares and on the wrong side of each one mark a diagonal line from corner to corner. Take one 9¼in print square and, RST, place a background square on two opposite corners, with the marked lines running from the corners towards the centre of the print square. The background squares will overlap in the centre. Sew ¼in either side of the marked lines. *Fig. A*

5. Cut the unit apart on the marked lines and press the two units open. *Fig. B*

6. Take one of the units from Step 5 and, RST, place a background square on the remaining print corner, with the marked line running from the print corner. Sew ¼in either side of the marked line. *Fig. C*

7. Cut the units apart on the marked line and press them open to complete two Large FG units, which should each measure 8½in × 4½in. *Fig. D*

Repeat with the remaining unit from Step 5 to make a total of four Large FG units.

8. Repeat Steps 4–7 with the remaining 9¼in print squares to make a total of sixty-four Large FG units.

9. Repeat Steps 4–7 with the 2⅞in background squares and 5¼in print squares to make a total of forty-eight Small FG Units.

Piecing the Diamond Units

10. Take two Large FG units of matching print fabrics and join to make one Large Diamond unit. *Fig. E*

11. Repeat Step 10 to make a total of twenty Large Diamond units.

12. Repeat Step 10 with two small FG units of matching print fabrics. Join a 4½in × 2½in background rectangle to the top edge and to the bottom edge of the unit to make one Small Diamond unit. *Fig. F*

13. Repeat Step 12 to make a total of fifteen Small Diamond units.

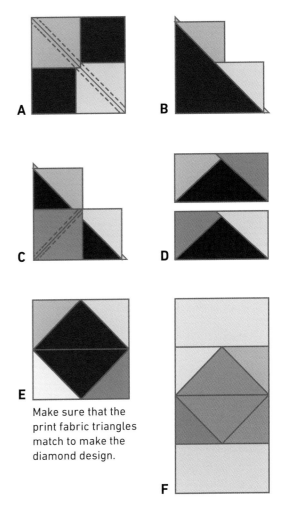

A **B**

C **D**

E

Make sure that the print fabric triangles match to make the diamond design.

F

Try different print placements to find that perfect layout.

Assembling the Quilt Top

14. Arrange the Large and Small Diamond units, the Large and Small FG units and the remaining 4½in × 2½in background rectangles into rows, experimenting with colour placement (layout diagram).

15. Join the 4½in × 2½in background rectangles to the bottom edges of the Small FG units. Join the units into rows, then join the rows to complete the quilt top.

Layout diagram

Quilting and Finishing

16. Cut the backing fabric in half across the width. Remove the selvedges and re-join the pieces along the length with a ½in seam. Press the seam open.

17. Press the quilt top and backing well. Make a quilt sandwich by placing the backing fabric right side down, the batting on top, then the quilt top centrally and right side up. The backing and batting are slightly larger than the quilt top. Baste the layers together using your preferred method.

18. Quilt as desired. Karen quilted a grid of rectangles across the quilt.

19. Trim off excess batting and backing fabric and square up the quilt.

20. Sew the binding strips together end-to-end using diagonal seams. Press the seams open and trim away the dog-ears. Fold in half lengthwise, WST, and press.

21. Sew the binding to the right side of the quilt, folding a mitre at each corner, then fold the binding over to the back of the quilt and hand stitch in place to finish.

SUN BAKED
Karen Lewis

Stitch up supersize blocks using intricate prints to make a quilt with plenty of texture and movement.

Try printing your own simple designs to complement fabrics from your stash.

PRINT PICK
Carolyn Friedlander's dreamy linen blend fabrics are perfect for these big blocks.

QUILT

Finished quilt:
50in × 70in approx

Fabrics used: Print fabrics are from the Euclid collection by Carolyn Friedlander for Robert Kaufman Fabrics, along with solids from the Brussels Linen collection, also by Robert Kaufman Fabrics, that Karen screen-printed.

You Will Need

Print fabrics: A total of approx 2yds

Background fabric (red print): 2yds

Backing fabric: 3¼yds

Batting: 56in × 76in

Binding fabric: ½yd

NOTES

- Seam allowances are ¼in, unless otherwise noted.
- Press seams open, unless otherwise instructed.
- FG = Flying Geese
- HST = half-square triangle
- RST = right sides together
- WOF = width of fabric
- WST = wrong sides together
- Fabric provided by Robert Kaufman Fabrics (robertkaufman.com)

Cutting Out

1. From the print fabrics cut:

- Forty (40) 5⅞in squares
- Five (5) 11½in squares
- Ten (10) 3in × 10½in rectangles

2. From the background fabric cut:

- Ten (10) 11¼in squares
- Five (5) 11½in squares
- Five (5) 5½in × 10½in rectangles

3. From the binding fabric cut seven (7) 2½in × WOF strips.

Piecing the FG Rows

4. Take four 5⅞in print squares and on the wrong side of each one mark a diagonal line from corner to corner.

5. Take one 11¼in background fabric square and, RST, place a 5⅞in print square on two opposite corners, with the marked lines running towards the centre of the background fabric square. The print squares will overlap where they meet in the centre. Sew ¼in either side of the marked line. *Fig. A*

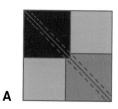

A

6. Cut the unit apart on the marked lines and press the two units open. *Fig. B*

7. Take one of the units from Step 6 and one of the remaining 5⅞in print squares. Place the print square on the remaining background fabric corner, RST and with the marked line running towards the centre. Sew ¼in either side of the marked line. *Fig. C*

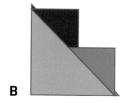

B

Repeat with the remaining unit from Step 6 and the remaining 5⅞in print square.

8. Cut the units apart on the marked lines. Press the units open to complete four Flying Geese units, which should each measure 10½in × 5½in. *Fig. D*

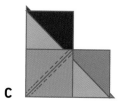

C

9. Repeat Steps 4–7 to make a total of forty FG units.

10. Take ten FG units and join them into a row, with all the units pointing towards the right, to complete Row 1.

11. Repeat Step 10 to make Row 4 and Row 6.

12. Take the ten remaining FG units and join them into pairs, with the central background fabric triangles facing each other. *Fig. E*

Join the pairs into a row to complete Row 2.

D

Piecing the HST Rows

13. Take one 11½in background fabric square and one 11½in print square. On the wrong side of the lighter square mark a line from

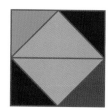

E

Make sure that the background triangles are facing each other.

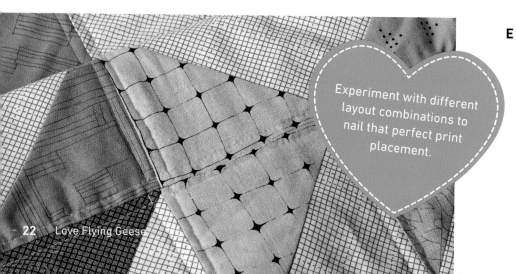

Experiment with different layout combinations to nail that perfect print placement.

corner to corner. Place the squares RST, with the marked square on top. Stitch ¼in either side of the marked line and then cut through both layers on the marked line. *Fig. F*

14. Open the units out and press. Keeping the 45-degree line of your ruler aligned with the diagonal seam, trim both units to 10½in square to make two HSTs. *Fig. G*

15. Repeat Steps 13 and 14 to make a total of ten HSTs.

16. Take five HSTs and join them into a row, with the diagonal seam running from bottom left to top right and with the print triangles on the left-hand side of this seam, to complete Row 3.

17. Take the five remaining HSTs and join them into a row, with the diagonal seam running from top left to bottom right and with the print triangles on the right-hand side of this seam, to complete Row 7.

Piecing the Rectangle Rows

18. Take one 5½in × 10½in background fabric rectangle and sew a 3in × 10½in print rectangle to each long edge to make one 10½in block. Repeat to make a total of five blocks.

19. Join the blocks into a row, alternating the orientation of adjacent blocks, to complete Row 5.

Assembling the Quilt Top

20. Take Rows 1–7 and arrange them as shown (layout diagram). Join the rows to complete the quilt top.

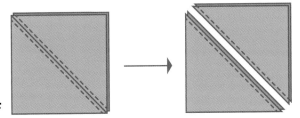

F

Mix and match different print fabrics for each pair of HSTs.

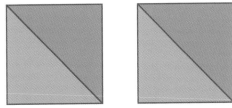

G

Keep the diagonal seam aligned with the 45-degree line on your ruler when trimming to keep the unit centred.

Layout diagram

Quilting and Finishing

21. Cut the backing fabric in half across the width. Remove the selvedges and re-join the pieces with a ½in seam. Press the seam open.

22. Press the quilt top and backing well. Make a quilt sandwich by placing the backing fabric right side down, the batting on top, then the quilt top centrally and right side up. Baste the layers together.

23. Quilt as desired. Karen quilted straight lines echoing the shapes in each unit.

24. Join the binding strips together end-to-end using diagonal seams. Press the seams open and trim away the dog-ears, then fold in half lengthwise, WST, and press.

25. Sew the binding to the front of the quilt, folding a mitre at each corner, then fold it over to the back of the quilt and hand stitch in place to finish.

GO GREEN
Invest in some cute succulents to match this quilt's natural vibe.

FANCY FLORA · Karen Lewis

Channel the botanical trend with layers of Flying Geese units featuring lush floral prints.

QUILT

Finished quilt: 50in × 84in

Fabrics used: Feature print fabrics are from the Outback Wife collection by Gertrude Made for Ella Blue Fabrics. Background print fabrics are from the Blueberry Park collection by Karen Lewis for Robert Kaufman Fabrics.

You Will Need

Blue feature prints: 1yd

Pink feature prints: 1yd

Yellow feature prints: 1yd

Blue background prints: 1¼yds

Pink background prints: 1yd

Yellow background prints: 1yd

Backing fabric: 5yds

Batting: 56in × 90in

Binding fabric: ½yd

Seventy (70) copies of the FPP template (page 28)

NOTES

- Seam allowances are ¼in, unless otherwise noted.
- Press seams open, unless otherwise instructed.
- FPP = foundation paper piecing
- RST = right sides together
- WOF = width of fabric
- WST = wrong sides together
- Fabric provided by Ella Blue Fabrics

Preparation

1. Trace the Section 1 and Section 4 Triangle Templates (page 28) onto card or template plastic and cut them out.

Use a variety of prints for your background fabrics to give a scrappy finish.

Cutting Out

2. From each of the feature print fabrics cut four (4) 4in × WOF strips and four (4) 3in × WOF strips.

3. Take one 3in × WOF feature print strip and place it wrong side up. Place the Section 1 Triangle template on top and draw around it, then rotate the template and draw around it again. *Fig. A*

Repeat to the end of the strip, then cut them out. You should get seven (7) from each strip.

4. Repeat Step 3 with the remaining 3in × WOF feature print strips to cut a total of the following:

- Twenty-five (25) blue feature print Section 1 triangles
- Twenty-three (23) pink feature print Section 1 triangles
- Twenty-two (22) yellow feature print Section 1 triangles

5. Repeat Step 3 with the 4in × WOF feature print strips and the Section 4 Triangle template to cut the following:

- Twenty-five (25) blue feature print Section 4 triangles
- Twenty-three (23) pink feature print Section 4 triangles
- Twenty-two (22) yellow feature print Section 4 triangles

6. From the blue background print fabrics cut five (5) 4½in × WOF strips and five (5) 3½in × WOF strips.

7. From both of the pink background print fabrics and the yellow background print fabrics cut four (4) 4½in × WOF strips and four (4) 3½in × WOF strips.

8. Take one 3½in × WOF background print strip and mark 7in rectangles along its length. Mark a diagonal line from the top left corner to bottom right corner (Section 2) on half of the rectangles and then mark a diagonal line from the bottom left corner to the top right corner (Section 3) on the remaining rectangles. *Fig. B*

A

B

Cut along all the marked lines to cut a total of six (6) Section 2 triangles and six (6) Section 3 triangles.

9. Repeat Step 8 with the remaining 3½in × WOF background print strips to cut a total of the following:

- Twenty-five (25) blue background print Section 2 triangles
- Twenty-five (25) blue background print Section 3 triangles
- Twenty-three (23) pink background print Section 2 triangles
- Twenty-three (23) pink background print Section 3 triangles
- Twenty-two (22) yellow background print Section 2 triangles
- Twenty-two (22) yellow background print Section 3 triangles

10. Repeat Step 8 with the 4½in × WOF background print strips to cut the following:

- Twenty-five (25) blue background print Section 5 triangles.
- Twenty-five (25) blue background print Section 6 triangles.
- Twenty-three (23) pink background print Section 5 triangles.
- Twenty-three (23) pink background print Section 6 triangles.
- Twenty-two (22) yellow background print Section 5 triangles.
- Twenty-two (22) yellow background print Section 6 triangles.

11. From binding fabric cut seven (7) 2½in × WOF strips.

Piecing the Blocks

12. Take one FPP template and one each of blue print triangles Sections 1–6. If you've used multiple prints, make sure that the feature fabric triangles match and that the background fabric triangles match.

13. To piece the template, place the Section 1 triangle right side up against Section 1 on the unprinted side of the template, making sure that the edges of the fabric extend at least ¼in all around the marked lines of Section 1. Pin in place.

14. Place the Section 2 triangle right side down on the Section 1 triangle, matching up the raw edges where Sections 1 and 2 will be joined. Check that when flipped over at the seamline the new fabric will cover Section 2 plus at least ¼in all around.

15. Turn the template over and stitch on the marked line between Sections 1 and 2, extending it by a few stitches at each end of the seam. Fold the template back and trim the seam allowance to ¼in. Flip the Section 2 triangle open and press.

16. Repeat Steps 12–15 to add the remaining sections in numerical order. Press and then trim the block on the outer dashed line of the template. Remove the template to complete one block.

17. Repeat Steps 12–16 to make a total of the following:

- Twenty-five (25) blue blocks
- Twenty-three (23) pink blocks
- Twenty-two (22) yellow blocks

Assembling the Quilt Top

18. Arrange the blocks into five vertical columns of fourteen blocks each, referring to the photo for orientation. Join the blocks into columns, then join the columns to complete the quilt top.

Quilting and Finishing

19. Cut the backing fabric in half across the width. Remove the selvedges and re-join the pieces with a ½in seam.

20. Press the quilt top and backing well. Make a quilt sandwich by placing the backing fabric right side down, the batting on top, then the quilt top centrally and right side up. Baste the layers together using your preferred method.

21. Quilt as desired. Karen quilted straight horizontal lines at varying intervals.

22. Trim off the excess batting and backing fabric and square up the quilt.

23. Join the binding strips together end-to-end using diagonal seams. Press the seams open then fold in half lengthwise, WST, and press.

24. Sew the binding to the front of the quilt, folding a mitre at each corner, then fold it over to the back of the quilt and hand stitch in place to finish.

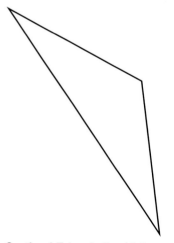

Section 1 Triangle Template: Enlarge 400%.

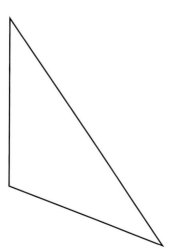

Section 4 Triangle Template: Enlarge 400%.

FPP Template: Enlarge 400%.

COLOUR STUDY 2
Karen Lewis

Whip up some luscious green Flying Geese units to create a contrast-colour quilt using precious prints from your stash.

SOLID IMPACT
Choose a lovely textured linen-look fabric to give your quilt added texture!

QUILT

Finished quilt: 60in × 80in

Fabrics used: A variety of green and yellow fabrics from Karen's stash along with Essex Yarn Dyed linen in Graphite, provided by Robert Kaufman Fabrics (robertkaufman.com).

You Will Need

Print fabrics: Twenty-eight (28) 11in squares

Background fabric: 4yds

Backing fabric: 70in × 90in

Batting: 70in × 90in

Binding fabric: ⅝yd

NOTES

- Seam allowances are ¼in thoroughly, unless otherwise noted.
- Press seams open, unless otherwise instructed.
- WOF = width of fabric
- HST = half-square triangle

Connect Flying Geese units in contrast shades.

Cutting Out

1. From each of the print fabrics cut one (1) 10½in × 5½in rectangle and two (2) 5½in squares.

2. From the background fabric cut the following:

- Forty-six (46) 10½in × 5½in rectangles
- Eleven (11) 10½in squares
- Fifty-six (56) 5½in squares

3. From the binding fabric cut eight (8) 2½in × WOF strips.

Making the Block

4. Mark a diagonal line on the reverse of all your 5½in squares.

5. Place a background fabric square, RST at one end of a print 10½in × 5½in rectangle. Sew along the diagonal, and trim ¼in from the sewn line. Press the corner open. *Fig. A*

6. Repeat Step 5 on the other end of the print rectangle to make one Flying Geese unit. *Fig. B*

Repeat to make twenty-eight (28) print fabric Flying Geese units using background squares.

7. Repeat Steps 4–6 to make twenty-eight (28) background Flying Geese units using background fabric 10½in × 5½in rectangles and matching print fabric 5½in squares.

8. Join matching background and print Flying Geese units along the long edges to form a print chevron. *Fig. C*

Repeat with all twenty-eight sets of Flying Geese.

Assembling the Quilt

9. Arrange the chevron blocks and remaining background pieces as shown (layout diagram). Sew each column together, pressing seams toward the background fabric.

10. Sew the columns together, pressing seams open, to finish the quilt top.

A

B

C

Alternate the direction of your units in each row to give a sense of movement.

Layout diagram

Quilting and Finishing

11. Cut your backing fabric in half and sew together along the long edges using a ½in seam. Make a quilt sandwich of the backing fabric, the batting and the quilt top. Pin or spray baste together.

12. Quilt as desired. Karen quilted in horizontal lines and diagonal lines to echo the chevron pattern.

13. Trim excess batting and backing and square up the quilt. Join the binding strips into one long length and press in half. Bind the quilt, carefully mitring each corner.

GAGGLE OF GEESE   Jeni Baker

Master Flying Geese with this striking quilt.

TECH FOCUS ...
This quilt is made up of
35 large and 140 small Flying
Geese units. Refer to the two
different making-up techniques
(page 37) as needed.

QUILT

Finished quilt:
50in × 70in approx

Fabrics used: Urban Mod prints and Pure Element Snow by Art Gallery Fabrics

You Will Need

Print fabrics: A fat quarter each of twenty prints

White solid fabric: 3yds

Cotton batting: 1¾yds of 90in wide

Backing fabric: 3¼yds

Binding fabric: 1½yds

NOTES
- Seam allowances are ¼in unless otherwise noted.
- WOF = width of fabric

Cutting Out

1. From each of five print fat quarters: Cut two 3in × 21in strips. Subcut each strip into seven 3in squares (70 in total). Cut one 5½in × 21in strip. Subcut the strip into two 5½in squares (ten in total).

2. From each of fifteen print fat quarters: Cut two 3in × 21in strips. Subcut each strip into seven 3in squares (210 in total). Cut one 5½in × 21in strip. Subcut the strip into three 5½in squares (45 in total). Cut one 5½in square (fifteen in total).

3. From white solid fabric: Cut five 10½in × WOF strips. Subcut each strip into seven 10½in × 5½in rectangles (35 in total). Cut ten 5½in × WOF strips. Subcut each strip into

fourteen 5½in × 3in rectangles (140 in total).

4. From binding fabric cut seven 2½in × WOF strips.

The green and blue in the backing fabric is a perfect pairing for the quilt top!

Making the Flying Geese Units

5. The quilt is made up of a total of 35 large and 140 small Flying Geese units. The large units have a finished size of 5½in × 10½in, and the small units a finished size of 3in × 5½in. See the Traditional Method (page 37) for making the units, or try the No-Waste Method (page 38). The illustrations show the basic process. Figs. A–H

6. For each large Flying Geese unit use two 5½in print squares and one 5½in × 10½in solid rectangle to make a total of 35 large Flying Geese units.

7. For each small Flying Geese unit use two 3in print squares and one 3in × 5½in solid rectangle to make a total of 140 small Flying Geese units.

8. Sew the small Flying Geese units together into pairs and press seams open or to one side, as preferred. Arrange the pairs into blocks with four Flying Geese units in each. Sew the pairs together and press seams open. Create 35 blocks in this way.

Assembling the Quilt Top

9. Arrange the large Flying Geese units and small Flying Geese units alternately into fourteen rows of five blocks each, as shown. Sew the blocks together into rows, pressing the seams in even-numbered rows in one direction, and the seams of odd-numbered rows in the opposite direction, so the row seams will nest together neatly.

10. Now sew the rows together, matching seams neatly and press the seams in one direction. The quilt top should measure 50½in × 70½in.

Quilting and Finishing

11. Cut the pressed backing yardage in half and trim off the selvedges. Sew the pieces together length-wise and press the seam open.

12. Make a quilt sandwich of the backing fabric (right side down), the batting and the quilt top (right side up). Baste or pin the layers together.

13. Quilt as desired. Once quilted, trim off excess backing fabric and batting and square up the quilt.

14. Prepare the binding by sewing the seven strips into one long length. Fold along the length, wrong sides together, and press. Use to bind the quilt.

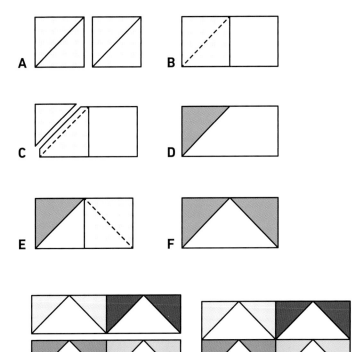

Layout diagram

Illustrations © Jeni Baker

MUG RUG

Finished mug rug:
6½in × 9½in approx

Just right for a cuppa and a biscuit.

NOTES

• Seam allowances are ¼in unless otherwise noted.

Cutting Out

1. From each print scrap cut two 2in squares (24 in total).

2. From white solid fabric cut one 2in × width of fabric strip. Subcut the strip into twelve 3½in × 2in rectangles.

3. From binding fabric cut one 2½in × width of fabric strip.

Making the Flying Geese Units

4. The mug rug is made up of twelve Flying Geese units, each with a finished size of 2in × 3½in. See the Traditional Method (next page) for making the units. For each Flying Geese unit use two 2in print squares and one

2in × 31½in solid rectangle. The illustrations below show the process. Make twelve Flying Geese in total. *Figs. A & B*

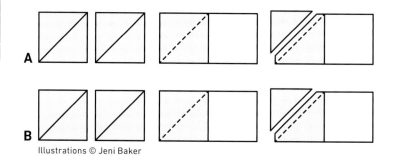

Illustrations © Jeni Baker

Assembling the Mug Rug

5. Arrange the Flying Geese units into six rows of two blocks each. Sew the blocks together in each row, pressing the seams in the first row in the opposite direction to the second row, so the row seams will nest together neatly.

6. Sew the rows together and press the seams in one direction. The mug rug should measure 6½in × 9½in.

Quilting and Finishing

7. Make a quilt sandwich of the backing fabric (right side *down*), the batting and the mug rug top (right side *up*). Baste or pin the layers together.

8. Quilt as desired. Once quilted, trim off excess backing fabric and batting and square up the mug rug.

9. Fold the binding strip along the length, wrong sides together and press. Use this doubled strip to bind the mug rug.

TECHNIQUE FOCUS: FLYING GEESE

The Flying Geese unit is key to many quilt designs—and forms a core part of your quilting arsenal. Here we share with you two techniques for making the perfect Flying Geese, with instructions by Jeni Baker.

Traditional Method

Makes one at a time.

CALCULATING FABRIC SIZES

- Finished Flying Geese: 2½in × 5in (height × width)
- Size of solid rectangle = (height + ½in) × (width + ½in) = (2½in + ½in) × (5in + ½in) = 3in × 5½in
- Size of print fabric squares = (height + ½in) × (height + ½in) = (2½in + ½in) × (2½in + ½in) = 3in × 3in

A

1. For one Flying Geese unit, cut one 3in × 5½in solid fabric rectangle and two 3in squares from print fabric. *Fig. A*

2. Using a water-soluble marker or pencil, mark a diagonal line across the wrong side of both print squares. *Fig. B*

3. Place one square in the right-hand corner of the solid rectangle, right sides together, as pictured. *Fig. C*

4. Stitch across the corner along the line you marked. *Figs. D & E*

5. Trim off excess fabric at the corner, lining up the ¼in line on your ruler with the stitching line to give you a ¼in seam. *Fig. F*

6. Press the corner up to form a triangle. *Fig. G*

7. Place the second print square in the left-hand corner of the solid rectangle, right sides together, as pictured. Repeat Steps 4–6 to complete the Flying Geese unit. Check the finished unit is 2½in × 5in. *Figs. H & I*

B

C

D

E

F

G

H

I

Step photography © Jeni Baker

No-Waste Method

Makes four at a time.

1. Cut one 6¼in solid square and four 3⅜in print squares. *Fig. A*

2. Using a water-soluble marker or pencil, mark a diagonal line across the wrong side of all the print squares. *Fig. B*

CALCULATING FABRIC SIZES
- Finished Flying Geese: 2½in × 5in (height × width)
- Size of solid fabric square: (width + 1¼in) × (width + 1¼in) = (5in + 1¼in) × (5in + 1¼in) = 6¼in × 6¼in
- Size of print fabric squares: (height + ⅞in) × (height + ⅞in) = (2½in + ⅞in) × (2½in + ⅞in) = 3⅜in × 3⅜in

3. Place one print square in the bottom right-hand corner of the solid square and one in the top left-hand corner, as pictured. Pin in place. *Fig. C*

4. Sew ¼in on either side of the marked line. *Figs. D & E*

5. Cut the square apart along the marked line. *Fig. F*

6. Press the print pieces away from the solid. *Fig. G*

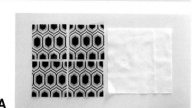

A

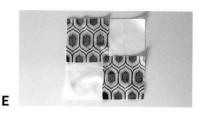

B

C

D

E

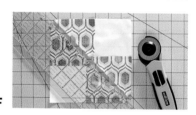

F

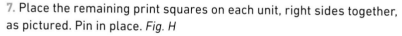

G

7. Place the remaining print squares on each unit, right sides together, as pictured. Pin in place. *Fig. H*

8. Sew ¼in on either side of the marked line. *Figs. I & J*

9. Cut apart along the marked line. *Fig. K*

10. Press the print pieces away from the solid. Trim off excess fabric. Check that the finished units are each 2½in × 5in. *Figs. L & M*

Your print squares will overlap when positioned—don't worry, they're meant to

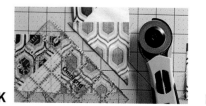

H

I

J

K

L

M

Step photography © Jeni Baker

MODERN CLASSICS
Brush up on your trad piecing with classic half-square triangles, Square-in-Square blocks and Flying Geese. They're eternally popular for a reason.

DESERT CROSSING Nicole Calver

Mix it up with trad motifs in these three mini quilt and supersize block sets.

COYOTE SUPERSIZE BLOCK

Finished supersize block:
24in square

Fabrics used: All print fabrics are from the Coyote collection by Hawthorne Threads. Fabric A: Golden print. Fabric B: Low-volume feather print. Fabric C: Coral print. Fabric D: Grey arrows on white print. Fabric E: White arrows on grey print. Fabric F: Coyote print.

You Will Need

For the Coyote supersize block:

Fabric A: One (1) FQ

Fabric B: One (1) FQ

Fabric C: One (1) FQ

Fabric D: One (1) FQ

Fabric E: One (1) FQ

Fabric F: One (1) FQ

Backing fabric: 28in square

Batting: 28in square

Binding fabric: ¼yd

NOTES
- Seam allowances are ¼in, unless otherwise noted.
- FQ = fat quarter
- RST = right sides together
- WOF = width of fabric
- HST = half-square triangle

Cutting Out

1. From Fabric A cut four (4) 5in squares and eight (8) 4½in squares.

2. From Fabric B cut four (4) squares measuring 5in.

3. From Fabric C cut two (2) squares measuring 9½in.

4. From Fabric D cut eight (8) squares measuring 4⅞in.

5. From Fabric E cut eight (8) squares measuring 4½in.

6. From Fabric F cut one (1) square measuring 8½in (fussy cut, if desired).

7. From your binding fabric cut three (3) 2¼in × WOF strips.

Add texture with a variety of quilt patterns.

Piecing the Supersize Block

8. Take your 5in squares of Fabrics A and B and sew together using the 2-in-1 HST method (page 47). Square up to 4½in. Using your eight 4½in Fabric A squares, sew together with your HSTs in a simple four-patch block as shown. *Fig. A*

Make four of these blocks.

9. Following the instructions for the 4-in-1 Flying Geese (page 49) make eight identical geese using Fabrics C and D. Set four of the finished geese aside.

10. With the remaining four geese and your eight squares of Fabric E, make corner square triangles on each side of each goose unit as follows:

• Place one square on the left-hand side of your goose block and draw a diagonal line from corner to corner as shown. *Fig. B*

• Sew along the line and cut ¼in from the line. *Fig. C*

• Press the corner back and repeat on the opposite side of the goose. *Fig. D*

• Repeat to make four of these new Flying Geese blocks. Sew these new blocks to your four regular Flying Geese units as shown. *Fig. E*

11. Arrange the blocks and Fabric F square as shown in the quilt photo (previous page) and sew together as you would a Nine-Patch block.

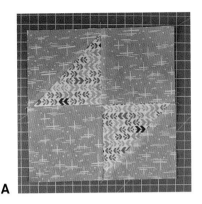

A

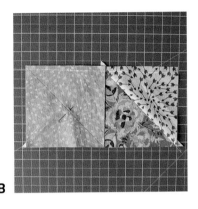

B

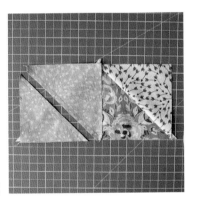

C

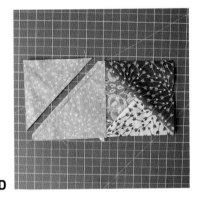

D

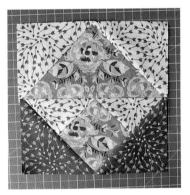

E

Quilting and Finishing

12. Baste and quilt as desired. Attach your preferred hanging device for mini quilts. Sew your binding strips end to end to form one length and use to bind the quilt.

COYOTE MINI QUILT

Finished mini quilt:
13½in square

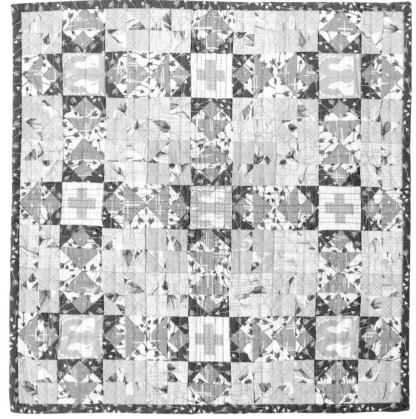

The mini uses smaller versions of the same Coyote blocks.

You Will Need

For the Coyote mini quilt:

Fabric A: One (1) FQ

Fabric B: One (1) FQ

Fabric C: One (1) FQ

Fabric D: One (1) FQ

Fabric E: One (1) FQ

Fabric F: One (1) FQ

Backing fabric: 17½in square

Batting: 17½in square

Binding fabric: ⅛yd

Cutting Out

1. From Fabric A cut seventy-two (72) 1¼in squares and thirty-six (36) 1¾in squares.

2. From Fabric B cut thirty-six (36) 1¾in squares.

3. From Fabric C cut eighteen (18) 2¾in squares.

4. From Fabric D cut seventy-two (72) 1⅝in squares.

5. From Fabric E cut seventy-two (72) 1¼in squares.

6. From Fabric F cut nine (9) 2in squares (fussy cut, if desired).

7. From your binding fabric cut two (2) 2¼in × WOF strips.

Piecing the Mini Quilt

8. Follow Steps 8–11 from the Coyote supersize block, trimming HSTs to 1¼in square. Repeat to make nine blocks and sew together as shown above. Baste and quilt the top as desired, then bind to finish.

With more piecing, it's best to use simple quilt lines.

DESERT ROSE SUPERSIZE BLOCK

Finished supersize block: 24in square

Fabrics used: All print fabrics are from the Coyote collection by Hawthorne Threads. Fabric A: White arrows on grey print. Fabric B: Golden coyote print. Fabric C: Coral geometric print. Fabric D: Darker coral print. Fabric E: Golden floral print.

You Will Need

For the Desert Rose supersize block:

Fabric A: One (1) FQ

Fabric B: One (1) FQ

Fabric C: One (1) FQ

Fabric D: One (1) FQ

Fabric E: One (1) FQ

Backing fabric: 28in square

Batting: 28in square

Binding fabric: ¼yd

Cutting Out

1. From Fabric A cut eight (8) squares measuring 4½in.

2. From Fabric B cut four (4) 8½in squares (fussy cut, if desired).

3. From Fabric C cut eight (8) 4½in squares and two (2) 9in squares.

4. From Fabric D cut two (2) squares measuring 9in.

5. From Fabric E cut one (1) square measuring 8½in.

6. From your binding fabric cut three (3) 2¼in × WOF strips.

Enhance the patchwork shapes with straight quilt lines at various widths apart to form a diamond.

Piecing the Supersize Block

7. Take your 9in Fabric C and D squares and sew together using the 2-in-1 HST method (page 47). You should have four HSTs. Square up each one to 8½in.

8. Following the instructions for the Square in Square units (page 48), use your 8½in squares of Fabric B as your base block and the 4½in squares of Fabrics A and C for the corners. When assembling, make sure you use the Fabric A squares at the bottom corners of your base block and the Fabric C squares at the top corners.

9. Arrange as shown above and sew together as for a Nine-Patch block.

Quilting and Finishing

10. Baste and quilt as desired, then bind the quilt to finish.

Take care to mitre the corners of your binding.

DESERT ROSE MINI QUILT

Finished mini quilt:
13½in square

Fabrics used: All print fabrics are from the Coyote collection by Hawthorne Threads. Fabric A: White arrows on grey print. Fabric B: Golden chevron print. Fabric C: Light coral prints. Fabric D: Dark coral prints. Fabric E: Low-volume floral print.

You Will Need

For the Desert Rose mini quilt:

Fabric A: One (1) FQ

Fabric B: One (1) FQ

Fabric C: One (1) FQ

Fabric D: One (1) FQ

Fabric E: One (1) FQ

Backing fabric: 17½in square

Batting: 17½in square

Binding fabric: ⅛yd

Cutting Out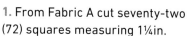

1. From Fabric A cut seventy-two (72) squares measuring 1¼in.

2. From Fabric B cut thirty-six (36) squares measuring 2in.

3. From Fabric C cut seventy-two (72) 1¼in squares and eighteen (18) 2½in squares.

4. From Fabric D cut eighteen (18) squares measuring 2½in.

5. From Fabric E cut nine (9) 2in squares (fussy cut, if desired).

6. From your binding fabric cut two (2) 2¼in × WOF strips.

Use different fabrics for four of the mini quilt blocks to create a cool contrast.

Piecing the Mini Quilt

7. Follow Steps 7–9 from the Desert Rose supersize block (page 43), trimming HSTs to 2in square. Repeat to make nine blocks and sew together as shown above. Baste and quilt the top as desired, then bind to finish.

These designs are so flexible, you could add more blocks to the mini quilt or combine it with the supersize block to make a larger quilt. Experiment!

Give a classic Star block a modern twist.

Make your quilt lines stand out with contrast thread.

DREAMCATCHER SUPERSIZE BLOCK

Finished supersize block:
24in square

Fabrics used: All print fabrics are from the Coyote collection by Hawthorne Threads. Fabric A: Multicoloured fussy-cut print. Fabric B: Aqua print. Fabric C: White arrows on grey print. Fabric D: Golden chevrons. Fabric E: Feathers print. Fabric F: Grey arrows on white print.

You Will Need

For the Dreamcatcher supersize block:

Fabric A: One (1) FQ

Fabric B: One (1) FQ

Fabric C: One (1) FQ

Fabric D: One (1) FQ

Fabric E: One (1) FQ

Fabric F: One (1) FQ

Backing fabric: 28in square

Batting: 28in square

Binding fabric: ¼yd

Plan carefully if you're using directional prints.

Using just one fat quarter of each print makes these designs great for trying out a new fabric collection.

Cutting Out

1. From Fabric A cut one (1) 8½in square (fussy cut, if desired).

2. From Fabric B cut twelve (12) squares measuring 4½in.

3. From Fabric C cut four (4) squares measuring 4⅞in.

4. From Fabric D cut one (1) 9½in square and four (4) 4⅞in squares.

5. From Fabric E cut four (4) squares measuring 8½in.

6. From Fabric F cut one (1) squares measuring 9½in.

7. From your binding fabric cut three (3) 2¼in × WOF strips.

Piecing the Supersize Block

8. Using your 8½in square of Fabric A and four of your 4½in squares of Fabric B, follow the instructions to make a Square in Square block (page 48).

9. Following the instructions for the 4-in-1 Flying Geese (page 49), make four identical geese using your Fabrics D and C together. Then make another set of four identical Flying Geese using your Fabrics F and D. Taking one of each different geese and sew together as shown. *Fig. A*

10. Take your remaining 4½in Fabric B squares and draw a diagonal line from corner to corner on the back. Place two of these squares RST on opposite corners of all four of your Fabric E squares. *Fig. B*

Note that if you are using a directional print for your base square (Fabric E), the placement of the corner squares will restrict the direction of your finished block. You may want to plan which corners you add your corner squares to. Sew along the line, then cut ¼in from the line. *Fig. C*

Repeat on opposite side and press open. *Fig. D*

11. Arrange the blocks as shown in the finished mini quilt (page 45) and sew together as you would a Nine-Patch block

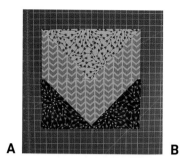

A

B

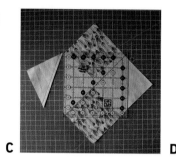

C

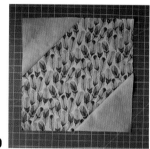

D

Quilting and Finishing

12. Baste and quilt as desired, then bind the quilt to finish.

DREAMCATCHER MINI QUILT

Finished mini quilt: 13½in square

Fabrics used: All print fabrics are from the Coyote collection by Hawthorne Threads. Fabric A: Fox print. Fabric B: Aqua prints. Fabric C: White arrows on grey. Fabric D: Golden print. Fabric E: Low volume print. Fabric F: Grey arrows on white.

Cutting Out

1. From Fabric A cut nine (9) 2in squares (fussy cut, if desired).

2. From Fabric B cut one hundred and eight (108) 1¼in squares.

3. From Fabric C thirty-six (36) 1⅝in squares.

4. From Fabric D cut thirty-six (36) 1⅝in squares and nine (9) 2¾in squares.

5. From Fabric E cut thirty-six (36) squares measuring 2in.

6. From Fabric F cut nine (9) squares measuring 2¾in.

7. From your binding fabric cut two (2) 2¼in × WOF strips.

Piecing the Mini Quilt

8. Repeat Steps 8–11 from the Dreamcatcher supersize block (page 46) nine times to make nine blocks. Sew together as shown (previous page).

Quilting and Finishing

9. Baste and quilt as desired, then bind the quilt to finish.

ESSENTIAL TECHNIQUES

2-in-1 HSTs

1. Take two squares and place them right sides together.

2. Draw a diagonal line from corner to corner.

3. Sew the squares together ¼in from the drawn line, on both sides.

TRADITIONAL TODAY
There's no better way to make a trad motif more modern than to blow it up in size! Or make it super-small. And don't forget the modern prints.

4. Cut along the corner-to-corner line you drew in Step 2. *Fig. A*

5. You will have created two HSTs. Press your two HSTs open. *Fig. B*

Square in Square

1. Draw a diagonal line from corner to corner on each of your corner squares.

2. Place two of your corner squares RST on top of your larger base square, lining them up at opposite corners. Position the corner squares so that the diagonal line you drew sits perpendicular to the corner.

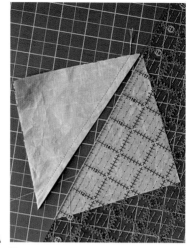

A

For a neat cut, place a quilt ruler on the line and trim with a rotary cutter on top of a cutting mat.

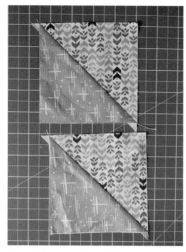

B

Using this method will give you two half-square triangles in double-quick time!

3. Stitch along the diagonal line. *Fig. C*

Then stitch ½in away from this line, towards the corner. This will yield one HST per corner.

4. Cut through both fabrics, in between your two sewn lines. *Fig. D*

5. Fold back the two corner pieces and press. *Fig. E*

6. Repeat Step 2 at the remaining two corners. *Fig. F*

7. Cut through both fabrics, in between your two sewn lines. Fold back the two sewn pieces and press to finish. *Fig. G*

C

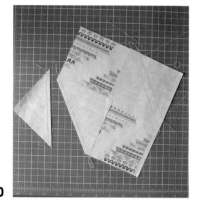

D

E

F

G

Making extra stitch lines when you create this block means you'll yield some extra HSTs for this project or another project.

4-in-1 Flying Geese

1. Place two small squares RST on your base square, at opposite corners. They should overlap slightly in the middle. Draw a diagonal line from corner to corner. *Fig. H*

2. Stitch a scant ¼in from your line, on both sides. Cut along the drawn line. *Fig. I*

3. Fold back the corners and press. You should have two identical units. *Fig. J*

4. Take another small square and place RST at the remaining corner of one unit. Draw a diagonal line from corner to corner. *Fig. K*

5. Stitch a scant ¼in from your line, on both sides. Cut along the drawn line. *Fig. L*

6. Press the corners back. You should have two Flying Geese. *Fig. M*

Repeat with the second unit to make two more Flying Geese.

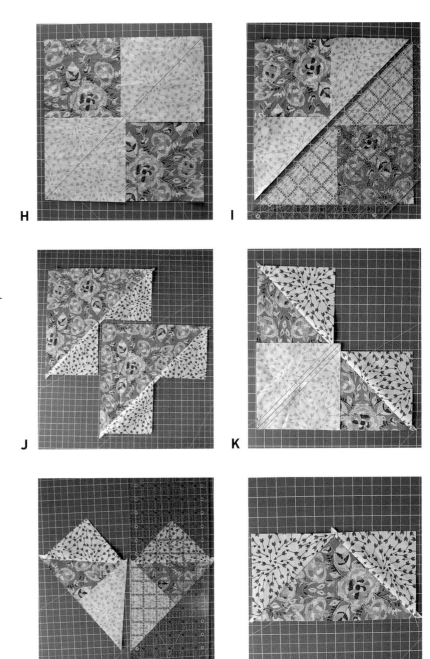

H   I

J   K

L   M

FEELING FRESH
Moira's striking arrow design and on-trend colour combos make a super fresh quilt.

ONWARD AND UPWARD
Moira de Carvalho

This Flying Geese quilt is perfect for showcasing your favourite fabrics in a modern design.

QUILT

Finished quilt:
64in × 72in approx

Fabrics used: Print fabrics are from the Imprint collection by Katarina Roccella for Art Gallery Fabrics.

You Will Need

Variety of print fabrics (Fabric A): A minimum of nine (9) different fat quarters

Pale fabric for background (Fabric B): 2½yds

Backing fabric: 72in × 80in (4yds approx)

Batting: 72in × 80in

Binding fabric: ½yd

NOTES

• Seam allowances are ¼in, unless otherwise stated.

• Press seams open, unless otherwise instructed.

• RST = right sides together

• WOF = width of fabric

• Wash and press all fabrics before cutting.

Cutting Out

1. From each Fabric A fat quarter cut:

• Two (2) 9¼in squares (eighteen total)

• Sixteen (16) 2½in squares (one hundred and forty-four total)

• Eight (8) 2½in × 4½in rectangles (seventy-two total)

2. From Fabric B (the pale background fabric) cut:

• Seventy-two (72) 4⅞in squares

• One hundred and forty-four (144) 2½in squares

• Seventy-two (72) 2½in × 4½in rectangles

3. From binding fabric cut seven (7) 2½in × WOF strips.

Making the Flying Geese Units

4. The Flying Geese are made using a four-at-once method, as follows. You will need one (1) Fabric A 9¼in square and four (4) Fabric B 4⅞in squares. Mark a diagonal line on the wrong side of each of the Fabric B squares.

5. Place a Fabric B square in the upper left corner of the Fabric A square, RST, as shown. *Fig. A*

Pin in place and then position another Fabric B square in the bottom right corner. Note that the two squares will overlap in the centre.

6. Sew on both sides of the marked lines using a ¼in seam. *Fig. B*

Cut the units apart along the marked lines. *Fig. C*

Press the units open.

7. Take one pressed unit and position one of the remaining Fabric B squares in the bottom left corner of the unit, with the diagonal line positioned between the two triangles, as shown. *Fig. D*

Sew on both sides of the marked line and then cut apart along the marked line. *Fig. E*

Press the units open and then check that the two Flying Geese units are 8½in × 4½in.

8. Repeat Step 7 with the remaining Flying Geese unit for a total of four (4) matching Flying Geese units. *Fig. F*

9. Use the remaining Fabric A 9¼in squares and Fabric B 4⅞in squares to make a total of seventy-two (72) Flying Geese units.

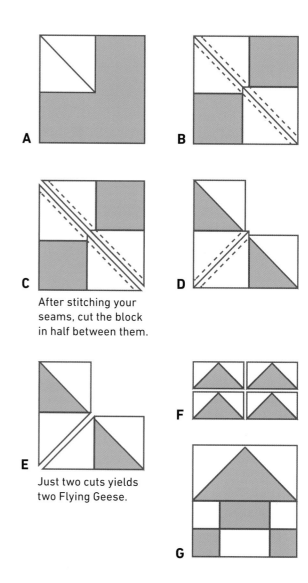

A   **B**

C   **D**
After stitching your seams, cut the block in half between them.

E   **F**
Just two cuts yields two Flying Geese.

G

TOP TIP
Before assembling your Flying Geese blocks, remember to trim off the "tails" and "ears" created by their construction. If you don't, you could create a bump in the seam when sewing them up.

The Four-at-Once Method for making Flying Geese blocks not only speeds up the process, but it also means that there's no waste from your fabric.

Assembling the Blocks

10. Referring to the illustration, lay out Fabric A and B 2½in squares and 2½in × 4½in rectangles. You will need two squares and one rectangle of each fabric. Make sure to use matching Fabric A pieces. Sew a Fabric B 2½in square to either side of a Fabric A 2½in × 4½in rectangle. Sew a Fabric A 2½in square to either side of a Fabric B 2½in × 4½in rectangle. Sew each of these units to a matching Flying Geese unit to complete the block. Press the block and check that it is 8½in square. *Fig. G*

11. Repeat this process with the remaining squares, rectangles and Flying Geese units to make a total of seventy-two (72) blocks.

Assembling the Quilt

12. Arrange the blocks in nine (9) rows, each with eight (8) blocks, alternating the direction of the 'arrows' in each row, as shown.

Layout diagram. Alternate the direction of your arrow blocks.

Sew the blocks into rows, pressing the seams in alternate directions. Now sew the rows together, matching seams neatly, and press.

Quilting and Finishing

13. Make a quilt sandwich by laying the backing fabric right side down, with the batting on top and then the quilt, right side up. Fix the layers together with pins or spray adhesive, or another method of your choice. Quilt as desired—Moira used a machine to quilt with simple wavy lines. When all quilting is complete, tidy all thread ends and then square up the quilt, trimming excess batting and backing fabric.

14. Sew the binding strips together end to end to form one long length. Fold and press in half, wrong sides together, all along the length. Sew the binding to the quilt, mitring the corners neatly. Hand or machine stitch the binding to the back of the quilt.

Wavy quilting lines break up the sharp arrows.

Squares are sewn to Flying Geese to create the arrows

A fabric with a clean print complements the block's shape.

SUMMER SCOOP

Peta Peace

Get ready for summer with supersize quilt blocks in sweet ice cream shades and a pop of hot pink!

STAND OUT
Bright coral prints contrast with the pastel palette for a bold finish.

QUILT

Finished quilt:
60in × 85in approx

Fabrics used: Print fabrics are from the Canyon collection by Kate Spain for Moda Fabrics.

You Will Need

Print fabric: Sixteen (16) fat quarters

White background fabric: 4½yds

Backing fabric: 5¼yds

Binding fabric: ½yd

Batting: 64in × 89in

NOTES

- Wash and press all fabrics well before cutting.
- Seam allowances are ¼in, unless otherwise noted.
- Press seams open, unless otherwise instructed.
- RST = right sides together
- WOF = width of fabric
- HST = half-square triangle
- Quilted by Diane's Quilting Quest

Blenders are the perfect choice, as they create texture within the blocks.

Cutting Out

1. Select four (4) print fat quarters to use for making both a full block and a partial block. From each of these cut three (3) 6¼in squares and twenty-four (24) 3in squares.

2. From each of the twelve (12) remaining print fat quarters cut two 6¼in squares and twenty (20) 3in squares.

TOP TIP

When cutting out the 6¼in and 3in print squares, keep squares of the same print together as one set. For a full block a print set requires two 6¼in squares and twenty 3in squares. For a partial block a print set requires one 6¼in square and four 3in squares.

3. From the white background fabric cut:

- Three (3) 5½in × WOF strips. Subcut to give a total of sixteen (16) 5½in squares.

- Six (6) 6¼in × WOF strips. Subcut to give a total of thirty-six (36) 6¼in squares.

- Twenty (20) 3in × WOF strips. Subcut to give a total of one hundred and thirty-six (136) 3in × 5½in rectangles.

- Three (3) 15½in × WOF strips. Subcut to give a total of sixteen (16) 15½in × 5½in rectangles.

4. From the binding fabric cut eight (8) 2¼in × WOF strips.

Making the Full Blocks

5. From one print fabric, take two 6¼in squares and twenty 3in squares. From the background fabric patches take one 5½in square, two 6¼in squares and eight 3in × 5½in rectangles—together these form one full block fabric set.

6. Take one 6¼in print square and one 6¼in background square. On the wrong side of the background square mark a diagonal line from corner to corner.

7. Place the squares RST with the marked square on top. Stitch ¼in either side of the marked line, then cut through both layers on the marked line. Open the units out and press.

8. Keeping the 45-degree line of your ruler aligned with the diagonal seam, trim to 5½in square. You will now have two identical HSTs. *Fig. A*

Repeat with the remaining 6¼in squares to give a total of four 5½in HSTs.

A

B

Trim off the corner of the fabric and then press open.

C

This geometric design is just a combination of half-square triangles and Flying Geese.

9. Take two 3in print squares and one 3in × 5½in background rectangle. On the wrong side of each square mark a diagonal line from corner to corner.

10. Working on one corner at a time, RST place a square on one corner of the rectangle, with the diagonal line running from the bottom corner to the top edge.

11. Stitch on the marked line and trim ¼in beyond the stitched line. Flip the corner open and press. Repeat for the other corner. *Fig. B*

This is a Flying Geese unit.

12. Repeat Steps 9–11 to make a total of eight Flying Geese units.

13. Pair up the Flying Geese units and join on a long edge, making sure that they are all pointing in the same direction. You will now have four 5½in Flying Geese squares.

14. Take the four remaining 3in print squares and, on the wrong side of each one, mark a diagonal line from corner to corner.

15. Take the 5½in background square and place it right side up. Right side down, place a 3in square on opposite corners of the large square, with the marked lines running from outer edge to outer edge of the large square—they will overlap in the centre.

16. Stitch on the marked lines and trim ¼in beyond the stitched lines, then flip the corners open and press. Repeat for the two remaining corners to complete the square-in-a-square unit. *Fig. C*

17. Lay out the HSTs and the Flying Geese squares into two rows of three units. *Fig. D*

Join, and then press seams as shown by the arrows. Repeat to make one row using the HSTs and the square-in-a-square units.

18. Join the three rows together to make one full 15½in square block, pressing the seams as shown. *Fig. E*

19. Repeat Steps 5–18 to make a total of sixteen full blocks.

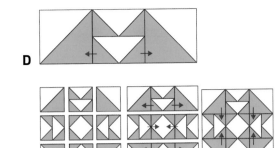

Making the Partial Blocks

20. From one print fabric, take one 6¼in square and four 3in squares. From the background fabric patches take one 6¼in square and two 3in × 5½in rectangles.

21. Make the two HSTs (Steps 6–8) and one 5½in Flying Geese square (Steps 9–11).

22. Join the units into a row to make one partial block, pressing seams outwards.

23. Repeat Steps 20–22 to make a total of four 15½in × 5½in partial blocks.

Piecing the Quilt Top

24. Join a 15½in × 5½in background rectangle to the top of each full block.

25. Lay out your full block / rectangle units and partial blocks, referring to the layout diagram for placement. Working in vertical columns, each column contains four full block / rectangle units and

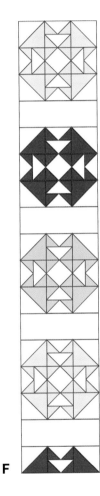

Layout diagram

one partial block, with the partial block alternating between top and bottom. Experiment with the placement of the prints and colours of your blocks to find your favourite design.

26. When you are happy with your layout, join the full block / rectangle units and partial blocks to make four vertical columns. *Fig. F*

Then join the columns together to complete the quilt top.

Quilting and Finishing

27. Cut the backing fabric in half across the width. Remove the selvedges and re-join the pieces along the length. The backing needs to be 2in bigger all around.

28. Make a quilt sandwich by placing the backing fabric right side down, the batting on top, then the quilt top centrally and right side up. The backing and batting are slightly larger than the quilt top. Baste the layers together using your usual method.

29. Quilt as desired. This quilt was quilted with a teardrop design.

30. Trim away any excess batting and backing, leaving an extra ⅛in of batting and backing beyond the quilt. This will help ensure that the binding is full and even on both the front and back of the quilt.

31. Sew the binding strips together end-to-end using diagonal seams.

32. Press the seams open, then fold in half lengthwise, WST, and press.

33. Sew the binding to the right side of the quilt, folding a mitre at each corner. Before completing your stitching, neaten the short raw end of the starting piece and insert the ending piece into it.

34. Fold the binding over to the back of the quilt and then hand stitch in place.

Teardrop quilting adds movement to the geometric design.

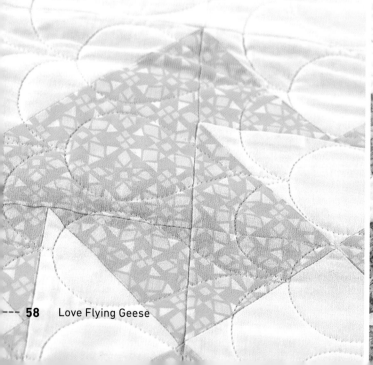

CUSHION

Finished cushion: 15in square approx

Fabrics used: Print fabrics are from the Canyon collection by Kate Spain for Moda Fabrics.

You Will Need

Print fabric: One (1) fat quarter

Background fabric: One (1) fat quarter

Calico lining fabric: 17in square

Coordinating backing fabric: ½yd

Binding fabric: One fat eighth

Batting: 17in square

Cushion pad: 15in square

Cutting Out

1. From the print fabric cut twenty (20) 3in squares and two (2) 6¼in squares.

2. From the background fabric cut:

• One (1) 5½in square

• Two (2) 6¼in squares

• Eight (8) 3in × 5½in rectangles

3. From the backing fabric cut two (2) 15½in × 19in rectangles.

4. From the binding fabric cut four (4) 2¼in × 21in strips.

Cushion Front

5. Follow Steps 5–18 of Making the Full Blocks (pages 56 and 57) to make one full block.

Quilting and Finishing

6. Make a quilt sandwich by placing the calico lining fabric right side down, the batting on top, then the cushion front centrally and right side up. The calico and batting are slightly larger than the cushion front. Baste the layers together using your preferred method.

7. Quilt as desired. Peta quilted diagonal lines approx 1in apart.

8. Trim away the excess batting and backing, leaving an extra ⅛in of batting and backing beyond the cushion front. This will make sure that the binding is full and even on both the front and back of the cushion.

9. Take the 15½in × 19in backing fabric rectangles and fold each one in half RST so each one measures 15½in × 9½in. Press.

10. Make the cushion back by arranging the two folded rectangles as shown so that they overlap by 3½in, with the folds in the centre and the raw edges on the outside.

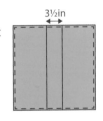

The rectangles will form a 15½in square. Pin to secure, then baste around the square using a ⅛in seam allowance.

11. Place the cushion front and back wrong sides together. Pin in place and baste around the edge of the cushion, using a scant ¼in seam allowance.

12. Follow Steps 31–34 (previous page) to sew the binding to the cushion front.

13. Fold the binding over to the back of the cushion and then hand stitch in place, then insert the cushion pad to finish.

14. To create the second cushion, you can swap the print and background fabrics in the cutting out instructions and the block construction to create the negative of the full block pattern.

DARK & LIGHT
Mix bold brights and candy pastel solids with shots of black for effortlessly modern style.

COLOUR TWIST
Nicole Calver

Give Flying Geese a clever update to make a high-contrast quilt with simple solid piecing.

QUILT

Finished quilt:
72in × 96in approx

Fabrics used: Solids are from the Cotton Supreme Solids collection for RJR Fabrics. Print fabrics are from the Fruit Dot collection by Melody Miller for Cotton + Steel.

You Will Need

Dark solids: ⅞yd each of six (6) different colours

Coordinating light solids: ⅝yd of six (6) different colours

Background fabric (black): 3⅛yds

Backing fabric: 5¾yds

Batting: 78in × 102in

Binding fabric: ¾yd

NOTES

• Seam allowances are ¼in, unless otherwise noted.

• WOF = width of fabric

• WST = wrong sides together

• FG = Flying Geese

Cutting Out

1. From each dark solid fabric cut four (4) 13¼in squares.

2. From each light solid fabric cut sixteen (16) 6½in squares.

3. From the background fabric cut ninety-six (96) 6⅞squares.

4. From your binding fabric cut nine (9) 2½in × WOF strips.

Making the Flying Geese

5. Take one 13¼in dark solid square and four 6⅞in background squares. RST, place a background square on opposite corners of the dark solid square then mark a diagonal line from corner to corner. *Fig. A*

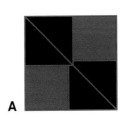

A

Try swapping the solid fabrics for ombré shades to give this quilt an on-trend tonal effect.

6. Stitch ¼in either side of the marked line and then cut apart on the marked line. *Fig. B*

Press the units open.

7. Mark a diagonal line on the wrong side of another background square. RST, place this square on the remaining corner of one of the units made in Step 6. *Fig. C*

8. Stitch ¼in either side of the marked line and then cut apart on the marked line. *Fig. D*

This will give you two Flying Geese units. Trim to 12½in × 6½in. *Fig. E*

9. Repeat Steps 7 and 8 with the other unit from Step 6 to give a total of four FG units.

10. Repeat Steps 5–9 with the remaining 13¼in dark solid squares and 6⅞in background squares. You will have sixteen FG units of each dark solid, giving a total of ninety-six FG units.

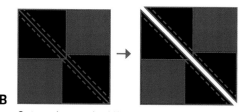

B

Cut on the marked line between your stitching.

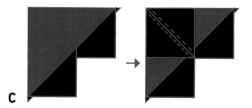

C

D

E

Piecing the Blocks

11. Put the FG units to one side. Take the sixteen 6½in light solid squares. On the wrong side of each one, draw a diagonal line from corner to corner, then draw another line ½in along, as shown. *Fig. F*

12. Take one FG unit and one light solid square in the coordinating colourway. Place the FG unit right side up with the point facing upwards. RST and matching up the raw edges, place the light square on the left-hand corner of the FG unit. The marked lines need to run from top left to bottom right—the shorter marked line will be the left-hand line.

13. Sew along both marked lines then cut apart between the stitched lines. *Fig. G*

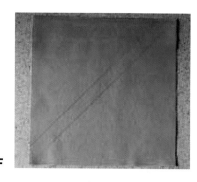

F

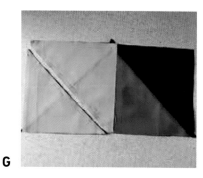

G

14. Open out the units and press. You will now have one Twisted FG unit for the quilt top and one quarter-square triangle style unit for use in another project. *Fig. H*

15. Repeat Steps 12–14 with the remaining FG units and light solid squares. You will now have sixteen Twisted FG units of each dark solid, giving a total of ninety-six Twisted FG units.

16. Take two Twisted FG units of the same colourway and join as shown. *Fig. I*

Your Twisted Flying Geese block should measure 12½in square.

17. Repeat Step 16 with your remaining Twisted FG units. You will have eight Twisted FG blocks of each colourway, giving a total of forty-eight Twisted FG blocks.

Assembling the Quilt Top

18. Arrange your blocks into eight rows of six blocks each, referring to the photo for placement and experimenting with the layout of the colours.

19. Join the blocks into rows and then join the rows to complete the quilt top.

Quilting and Finishing

20. Cut the backing fabric in half across the width. Remove the selvedges and re-join the pieces along the length with a ½in seam. Press the seam open.

21. Press the quilt top and backing. Make a quilt sandwich by placing the backing fabric right side down, the batting on top, then the quilt top centrally and right side up. The backing and batting are slightly larger than the quilt top. Baste the layers together.

22. Quilt as desired. Nicole quilted pairs of horizontal lines using variegated thread. Trim off any excess batting and backing fabric, and square up the quilt.

23. Sew the binding strips together end-to-end using diagonal seams. Press the seams open and trim away the dog-ears. Fold the binding in half lengthwise, WST, and press.

24. Sew the binding to the right side of the quilt, folding a mitre at each corner, then fold the binding over to the back of the quilt and hand stitch in place to finish.

H

I

Straight quilting accentuates the linear design.

CUSHION

Finished cushion: 18in square approx

You Will Need

Dark solids: One (1) fat eighth each of six (6) different colours

Coordinating light solids: One (1) fat eighth each of six (6) different colours

Background fabric (white): ½yd

Calico lining: 22in square

Backing fabric: ⅜yd

Batting: 22in square

A white background really shows off the variegated thread.

Cutting Out ✂

1. From each dark solid fabric cut three (3) 4¼in squares.

2. From each light solid fabric cut twelve (12) 2in squares.

3. From the background fabric cut seventy-two (72) 2⅜in squares.

4. From the backing fabric cut two (2) 18½in × 13in rectangles.

Making the Blocks

5. Repeat Steps 5–9 of Making the Flying Geese (pages 61 and 62) using the 4¼in dark solid squares and the 2⅜in background squares to make the FG units. You will make twelve units of each dark solid, making a total of seventy-two units, each measuring 3½in × 2in.

6. Repeat Steps 11–14 of Piecing the Blocks (pages 62 and 63) with the FG units from Step 5 and the 2in light solid squares to make the Twisted FG blocks. You will make six blocks of each colourway, making a total of thirty-six blocks, each measuring 3½in square.

Making the Cushion Top

7. Arrange your blocks into six rows of six blocks each, referring to the photo for placement.

8. Join the blocks into rows and then join the rows to complete the cushion top.

9. Make a quilt sandwich by placing the calico right side down, the batting on top, then the cushion top centrally and right side up. The backing and batting are slightly larger than the cushion top. Baste the layers together using your preferred method.

10. Quilt as desired. Nicole quilted diagonal lines in a variegated thread. Trim off any excess batting and calico, and square up the cushion top.

11. On one long edge of each 18½in × 13in backing fabric rectangle, turn over a ½in seam to the wrong side, then turn over another ½in and press. Top-stitch along the edge of the fold to secure.

12. Place the quilted cushion top right side up. Right side down, matching up the raw edges with the top edge and side edges of the cushion top, place one cushion back on top. The neatened seam will run across the width of the cushion top. Place the second cushion back in the same way, this time matching the raw edges with the bottom and side edges of the cushion top. The cushion back pieces will overlap. Pin or clip all around then join with a ¼in seam.

13. Clip the corners, taking care not to cut into the stitching. Turn the cushion cover right sides out and press, then insert the cushion pad to finish.

STAR CROSSED

Amanda Castor

Supersize some Flying Geese units in saturated shades to make a minimalist design with a textured background.

COLOUR CRUSH
Vibrant berry tones are so on-trend!

QUILT

Finished quilt:
45in × 58in approx

Fabrics used: Fabrics are from the Literary collection by Heather Givans for Windham Fabrics.

You Will Need

Purple fabric: ¼yd

Background fabric: 2¼yds

Backing fabric: 2⅞yds

Batting: 51in × 64in

Binding: ½yd

NOTES

- Seam allowances are ¼in, unless otherwise noted.
- Starch and press the fabric before cutting to avoid stretching the bias edges.
- FG = Flying Geese
- RST = right sides together
- WOF = width of fabric
- WST = wrong sides together

Choose a background fabric with a multidirectional print that will suit different angles.

Cutting Out

1. From the purple fabric cut two (2) 3⅞in × WOF strips. Subcut into sixteen (16) 3⅞in squares.

2. From the background fabric cut:

- One (1) 7¼in × WOF strip. Subcut into four (4) 7¼in squares.
- One 45in × WOF strip. Subcut into one (1) 8½in × 45in rectangle and one (1) 25½in × 45in rectangle.
- One (1) 25½in × WOF strip. Subcut into one (1) 14½in × 25½in rectangle and one (1) 6½in × 25½in rectangle.
- One (1) 17¾in square. Cut across both diagonals to give four (4) large triangles.
- Two (2) 6½in squares. Cut one of the squares across both diagonals to give four (4) small triangles.

3. From the binding fabric cut six (6) 2½in × WOF strips.

Making the FG Units

4. Take four 3⅞in purple squares and on the wrong side of each one mark a diagonal line from corner to corner. Take one 7¼in background square and, RST, place a purple square on two opposite corners, with the marked lines running towards the centre of the background square. The purple squares will overlap in the middle. Sew ¼in either side of the marked lines. *Fig. A*

5. Cut the unit apart on the marked lines and press the two units open. *Fig. B*

6. Take one of the units from Step 5 and, RST, place a purple square on the remaining background corner, with the marked line running towards the centre. Sew ¼in either side of the line. *Fig. C*

7. Cut the unit apart on the marked line. *Fig. D*

Press the two units open to complete two Flying Geese units. *Fig. E*

8. Repeat Steps 6 and 7 with the remaining unit from Step 5 and the remaining purple square. You will now have four FG units, which should each measure 6½in × 3½in.

9. Repeat Steps 4–8 to make a total of sixteen FG units.

Assembling the Quilt Top

10. Take four FG units and sew together into a row, making sure that all the units are pointing in the same direction. *Fig. F*

Repeat to make a total of four FG unit strips.

11. Take the following:

• Four (4) FG unit strips

• One (1) 6½in background square

• Four (4) large background triangles

• Four (4) small background triangles

Arrange as shown and then sew the units together as indicated by the arrows to complete the FG section of the quilt top, which should measure 25½in square. *Fig. G*

12. Sew the 6½in × 25½in background rectangle to the right-hand edge of the FG section and sew the

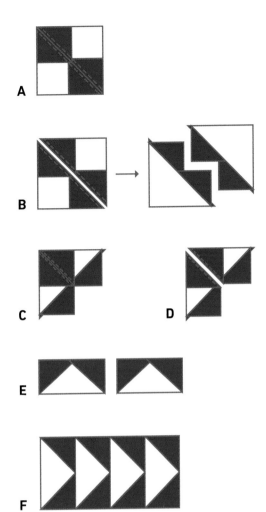

A

B

C   D

E

F

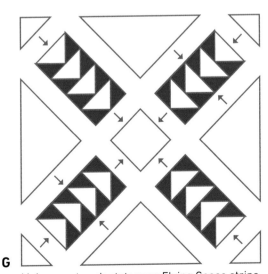

G

Make sure to orientate your Flying Geese strips correctly to create the cross shape.

14½in × 25½in background rectangle to the left-hand edge.

13. Sew the 45in × 8½in background rectangle to the bottom edge of the unit made in Step 12, and then sew the 45in × 25½in rectangle to the top edge as shown (layout diagram).

Quilting and Finishing

14. Cut the backing fabric in half across the width. Remove the selvedges and re-join the pieces along the length with a ½in seam. Press the seam open.

15. Press the quilt top and backing well. Make a quilt sandwich by placing the backing fabric right side down, the batting on top, then the quilt top centrally and right side up. The backing and batting are slightly larger than the quilt top. Baste the layers together using your preferred method.

16. Quilt as desired. Amanda quilted a combination of vertical, horizontal and diagonal straight lines.

17. Trim off excess batting and backing fabric and square up the quilt.

18. Sew the binding strips together end-to-end using diagonal seams. Press the seams open and trim away the dog-ears. Fold in half lengthwise, WST, and press.

19. Sew the binding to the right side of the quilt, folding a mitre at each corner, then fold the binding over to the back of the quilt and hand stitch in place to finish.

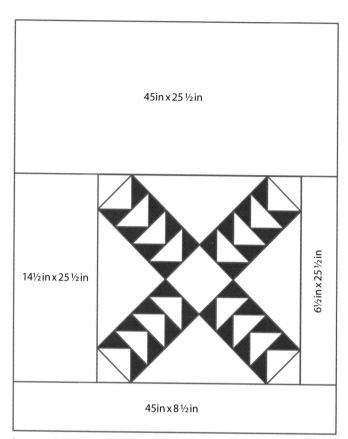

Layout diagram

In the diagram: 45in x 25 ½in; 14½in x 25 ½in; 6½in x 25½in; 45in x 8 ½in

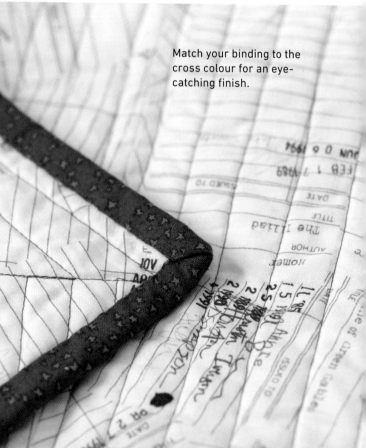

Match your binding to the cross colour for an eye-catching finish.

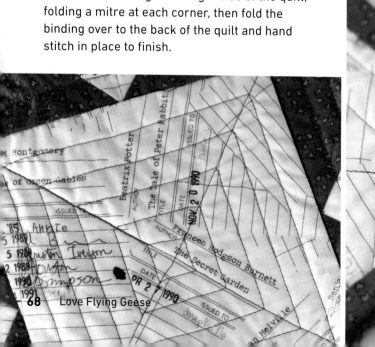

FOLKSY FLOCK

Jemima Flendt

*Make a statement by layering up colourful Flying Geese
of all different sizes into a quilt full of print and pattern.*

QUILT

Finished quilt:
72in × 80in approx

Fabrics used: Print fabrics are all from the Loominous Yarn Dyes I and II collections by Anna Maria Horner for FreeSpirit Fabrics in the following prints: Dotted Line in Coral, Cobalt, and Eggplant; Plenty in Berry, Wave, and Pine; Tribe in Bubblegum and Turquoise; Chemistry in Royal and Sharp; Checkered Past in Sky and Lantern; and Criss Cross in Mountain. Backing fabric is Sateen Solid in Cream from the Designer Sateen Solids collection by FreeSpirit Fabrics.

You Will Need

Background fabric (cream): 5⅝yds

Pink prints: ⅜yd each of four (4) different prints

Blue prints: ⅜yd each of four (4) different prints

Yellow prints: ⅛yd each of two (2) different prints

Aqua prints: ⅛yd each of two (2) different prints

Backing fabric: 4¾yds

Batting: 78in × 86in

Binding fabric: ¾yd

NOTES
- Seam allowances are ¼in, unless otherwise noted.
- FG = Flying Geese
- WOF = width of fabric
- WST = wrong sides together
- This quilt was professionally long-arm quilted by Carol Brady of The Quilting Cottage (carolbradyquilting.blogspot.com).

Use textured fabrics like this Loominous collection for a tactile finishing touch.

Cutting Out

1. From the background fabric cut:

- Eighteen (18) 3in × WOF strips. Subcut into two hundred and fifty-two (252) 3in squares.
- Twelve (12) 3in × WOF strips. Subcut into forty-six (46) 3in × 10½in rectangles.
- Twelve (12) 5½in × WOF strips. Subcut into eighty-one (81) 5½in squares.
- Two (2) 5½in × WOF strips. Subcut into seventeen (17) 5½in × 3in rectangles.
- Four (4) 5½in × WOF strips. Subcut into seventeen (17) 5½in × 8in rectangles.

2. From each of the pink prints cut two (2) 5½in × WOF strips. Subcut each strip into twenty-three (23) 5½in × 3in rectangles to give a total of ninety-two (92) rectangles.

3. From each of the blue prints cut two (2) 5½in × WOF strips. Subcut each strip into eight (8) 10½in × 5½in rectangles to give a total of thirty-two (32) rectangles.

4. From each of the yellow prints cut one (1) 3in × WOF strip. Subcut each strip into nine (9) 5½in × 3in rectangles to give a total of eighteen (18) rectangles. You need seventeen, so will have one left over.

5. From each of the aqua prints cut one (1) 3in × WOF strip. Subcut each strip into nine (9) 5½in × 3in rectangles to give a total of eighteen (18) rectangles. You need seventeen, so will have one left over.

6. From the binding fabric cut nine (9) 2½in × WOF strips.

Piecing Block A

7. Take one 5½in × 3in pink print rectangle and two 3in background squares.

8. On the wrong side of each square mark a diagonal line from corner to corner. With right sides together, place a square on one corner of the rectangle, with the diagonal line running from the bottom corner to the top long edge. *Fig. A*

9. Stitch on the marked line and trim then ¼in beyond the stitched line. Flip the corner open and press the seam towards the background triangle. *Fig. B*

Repeat on the other corner to complete one pink FG unit, which should measure 5½in × 3in. *Fig. C*

10. Repeat Steps 7–9 with the remaining pink print rectangles to make a total of ninety-two pink FG units.

11. Take one FG unit of each prink print. Arrange them in a column with each unit pointing upwards. Join, pressing the seams towards the pink prints. Take two 3in × 10½in background rectangles and join one to each side of the FG column. Press the seams outwards to complete one Block A, which should measure 10½in square. *Fig. D*

12. Repeat Step 11 to make a total of twenty-three of Block A.

Piecing Block B

13. Take one 10½in × 5½in blue print rectangle and two 5½in background squares. Repeat Steps 8 and 9 to make one blue FG unit, which should measure 10½in × 5½in.

14. Repeat Step 13 with the remaining blue print rectangles to make a total of thirty-two blue print FG units.

15. Take one FG unit of two different blue prints. Arrange in a column with each unit pointing upwards. Join, pressing the seam towards the blue print, to complete one Block B, which should measure 10½in square. *Fig. E*

16. Repeat Step 15 to make a total of sixteen of Block B.

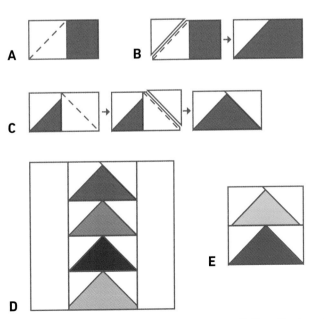

Piecing Block C

17. Take one 5½in × 3in yellow print rectangle and two 3in background squares. Repeat Steps 8 and 9 to make one yellow print FG unit, which should measure 5½in × 3in.

18. Repeat Step 17 with the remaining yellow print rectangles to make a total of seventeen yellow print FG units.

19. Take one 5½in × 3in aqua print rectangle and two 3in background squares. Repeat Steps 8 and 9 to make one aqua print FG unit, which should measure 5½in × 3in.

20. Repeat Step 19 with the remaining aqua print rectangles to make a total of seventeen aqua FG units.

21. Take the following:

• One (1) yellow FG unit

• One (1) aqua FG unit

• One (1) 5½in background square

• One (1) 5½in × 3in background rectangle

• One (1) 5½in × 8in background rectangle

Arrange the pieces as shown. *Fig. F*

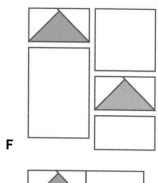

F

22. Join the pieces into columns, then join the two columns to complete one Block C, which should measure 10½in square. *Fig. G*

23. Repeat Steps 21 and 22 to make a total of seventeen of Block C.

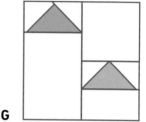

G

Assembling the Quilt

24. Take the blocks and arrange them into eight rows of seven blocks each, referring to the layout diagram for placement and experimenting with different layouts to get a good mix of colour and print across the quilt top (layout diagram).

25. Once you are happy with your layout, sew the blocks together into rows, then sew the rows together to complete the quilt top. Press the seams open.

Layout diagram

Quilting and Finishing

26. Cut the backing fabric in half across the width. Remove the selvedges and re-join the pieces along the length with a ½in seam. Press the seam open.

27. Press the quilt top and backing well. Make a quilt sandwich by placing the backing fabric right side down, the batting on top, then the quilt top centrally and right side up. The backing and batting are slightly larger than the quilt top. Baste the layers together using your preferred method.

28. Quilt as desired. This quilt was long-arm quilted with a curved design by Carol Brady of The Quilting Cottage.

29. Trim off excess batting and backing fabric and square up the quilt.

30. Join the binding strips together end-to-end using diagonal seams. Press the seams open and trim away the dog-ears, then fold in half lengthwise, WST, and press.

31. Sew the binding to the front of the quilt, folding a mitre at each corner, then fold the binding over to the back of the quilt and hand stitch in place to finish.

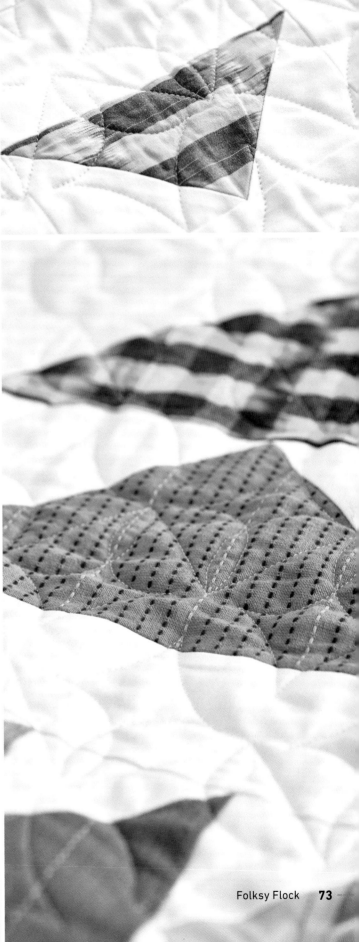

Curved quilting contrasts with the linear triangles.

Dear Diary
Minki Kim

Frame a fussy-cut square with a ripple of Flying Geese and Hourglass blocks, to make a quilt that's bursting with energy.

PRINT PLACEMENT
Lay out your pieced units to determine the flow of colour and pattern.

QUILT

Finished quilt: 55in × 65in

Fabrics used: Print fabrics are from the Dear Diary collection by Minki Kim for Riley Blake Designs.

You Will Need

Background fabric: 2yds

White print: ⅞yd

Print fabrics: At least eighteen (18) fat quarters

Batting: 60in × 70in

Backing fabric: 3½yds

Binding fabric: ½yd

Four (4) copies of the Flying Geese FPP template (page 77)

NOTES

- Seam allowances are ¼in throughout, unless otherwise noted.
- Adjust stitch length to 1.5 mm for FPP.
- Templates include outer seam allowances only.
- WOF = width of fabric
- RST = right sides together
- WST = wrong sides together
- HST = half-square triangles
- FPP = foundation paper piecing

Cutting Out

1. From the background fabric cut:
- Sixty four (64) 6½in squares

2. From the white print cut:
- Thirty two (32) 5in squares
- Four (4) 8½in squares

3. Choose four print fabrics and from each one cut:
- Four (4) 2½in × 4½in rectangles
- From one of these, also cut one (1) 4½in square.

4. From the remaining assorted prints, cut:
- Sixty four (64) 6½in squares

5. From the binding fabric cut:
- Seven (7) 2½in × WOF strips

Rotate a random selection of Hourglass blocks to add a little movement.

Hourglass Blocks

6. Mark a diagonal line on the wrong side of each background 6½in square.

7. Pair one 6½in background square with a 6½in print square, RST. Sew ¼in from either side of the drawn line. Cut along the line and press open to make two HST units.

A

8. Pair up the HSTs with opposite fabrics right sides together. *Fig. A*

Mark a drawn line perpendicular to the seam and sew ¼in from either side of the drawn line. Cut apart, press open and trim to 5½in square. *Fig. B*

9. Repeat Steps 8 and 9 with the remaining 6½in squares to make a total of one hundred and twenty seven (127) Hourglass blocks.

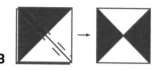

B

Assembling the Centre Unit

10. Foundation piece each of the Flying Geese FPP templates as follows. Use the print 2½in × 4½in rectangles for the large triangles and the white print 5in squares for the small triangles.

11. Place the fabric for Section 1 on the unprinted side of the template, so it covers all of Section 1, plus ¼in all the way around.

12. Place the fabric for Section 2 RST with the Section 1 fabric, with raw edges aligned along the line between Section 1 and 2. Check that when sewn, the fabric will cover all of Section 2 plus ¼in all the way around. Pin in place.

13. With the template printed side up, sew along the line between Section 1 and 2. Check the fabric will cover each section, then fold back the template along the seam and trim the seam to ¼in. Unfold the template and press the fabric open.

14. Repeat the last two steps, working in numerical order until the template is completely pieced. Piece all four templates in the same way, matching the

print fabrics for the large triangles to make four identical Flying Geese units.

15. Trim the templates along the outer dashed edge and remove the papers, tearing along the seamlines.

16. Arrange the Flying Geese units, print 4½in square and four white print 8½in squares as shown. *Fig. C*

Sew together in rows, then sew the rows together to complete the centre unit.

Assembling the Quilt Top

17. Arrange four rows of four Hourglass blocks, and four rows of three Hourglass blocks. Sew each set together in rows, then sew the rows together. Attach these units to either side of the centre unit. *Fig. D*

18. Arrange your remaining Hourglass blocks in nine rows of eleven. Sew the rows together.

19. Sew three of the hourglass rows together in one section. Sew the remaining six rows together in one section. Then sew each section to the top and bottom of the centre unit to complete the quilt top (layout diagram).

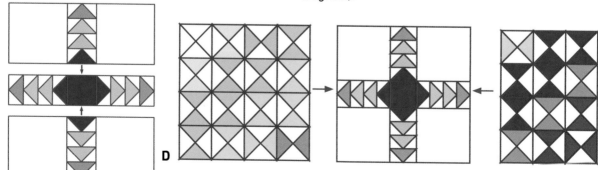

C

D

Finishing the Quilt

20. Cut your backing in half along the width. Sew together along the long edges using a ½in seam. Press open.

21. Press the quilt top and backing well. Make a quilt sandwich by placing the backing fabric right side down, the batting on top, then the quilt top centrally and right side up. The backing and batting are slightly larger than the quilt top. Baste the layers together using your preferred method.

22. Quilt as desired. Minki quilted straight lines either side of the seams.

23. Trim the excess batting and backing level with the quilt top edges and square up the quilt.

24. Sew the binding strips together end-to-end using diagonal seams. Press the seams open and trim away the dog-ears. Fold in half lengthwise, WST, and press.

25. Sew the binding to the right side of the quilt, folding a mitre at each corner. Fold the binding over to the back of the quilt and hand stitch in place to finish.

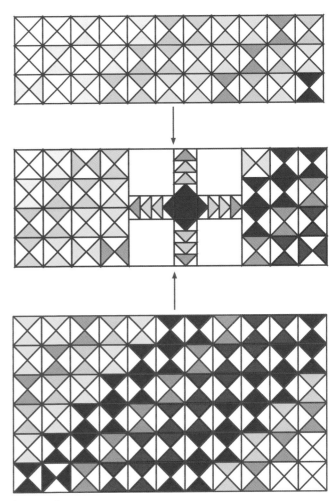

Layout diagram

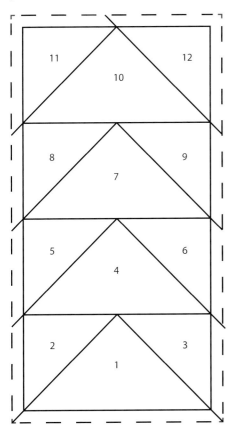

Flying Geese FPP: Enlarge 200%.

HEADING SOUTH

Amanda Castor

When autumn's on the way, keep things fresh and bright with this clever colour-combo quilt.

BALANCING ACT
A soft, leafy green is the perfect bridge for the hot and cold colours that Amanda's combined in her Flying Geese strips.

QUILT

Finished quilt:
64in × 68in approx

Fabrics used: Amanda used a selection of prints from her stash for the geese and Moda's Grunge Basics in Snow White for the background.

You Will Need

Orange print fabrics:
½yd total

Yellow print fabrics:
½yd total

Green print fabrics: ½yd total

Blue print fabrics: ½yd total

Grey print fabrics: ½yd total

Background fabric (white):
3½yds

Backing fabric: 4yds

Cotton batting: 72in × 76in

Binding: ½yd

NOTES
- All seam allowances are ¼in, unless otherwise noted.
- RST = right sides together
- WOF = width of fabric

Once you get into the swing of it you'll be piecing Flying Geese in no time!

Cutting Out

1. From each colour of print fabrics cut three (3) 9¼in squares (for the large Flying Geese units) and three (3) 5¼in squares (for the small Flying Geese units).

2. From the background fabric cut the following:

- Eight (8) 4⅞in × WOF strips. Subcut into sixty (60) 4⅞in squares (for the large Flying Geese units).

- Five (5) 2⅞in × WOF strips. Subcut into sixty (60) 2⅞in squares (for the small Flying Geese units).

3. From the background fabric cut three (3) 8½in × WOF strips and subcut as follows:

- Subcut strip 1 into one (1) 8½in × 18½in rectangle and two (2) 8½in × 10½in rectangles.

- Subcut strip 2 into one (1) 8½in × 22½in rectangle, two (2) 8½in × 4½in rectangles and one (1) 8½in × 6½in rectangle.

- Subcut strip 3 into one (1) 8½in × 12½in rectangle one (1) 8½in × 2½in rectangle and one (1) 8½in × 6½in rectangle.

4. From the background fabric cut seven (7) 4½in × WOF strips and subcut as follows:

- Subcut strip 1 into one (1) 4½in × 34½in rectangle.

- Subcut strip 2 into one (1) 4½in × 32½in rectangle, one (1) 4½in square and one (1) 4½in × 2½in rectangle.

- Subcut strip 3 into one (1) 4½in × 24½in rectangle and one (1) 4½in × 10½in rectangle.

- Subcut strip 4 into one (1) 4½in × 22½in rectangle and one (1) 4½in × 16½in rectangle.

- Subcut strip 5 into two (2) 4½in × 16½in rectangles.

- Subcut strip 6 into one (1) 4½in × 32½in rectangle.

- Use strip 7 and a scrap from one of the previous strips to create one (1) 4½in × 48½in rectangle.

- Use two (2) scraps from the previous strips to create one (1) 4½in × 16½in rectangle.

5. From the background fabric cut four (4) 2½in × WOF strips. Join these together into one long length and then cut two (2) strips each 2½in × 68½in.

6. From the binding fabric cut seven (7) 2½in × WOF strips.

Making the Flying Geese Blocks

7. To create the large Flying Geese blocks, select one 9¼in print fabric square and four 4⅞in background fabric squares. *Fig. A*

8. With RST place two of the background squares on the larger print fabric square as shown. *Fig. B*

Using a ruler, draw a diagonal line from the top left corner to the bottom right corner. Stitch ¼in on each side of the drawn line. *Fig. C*

Cut apart directly on the drawn diagonal line. *Fig. D*

Press seams towards the background fabric. *Fig. E*

9. With RST, place one 4⅞in background square on the sewn unit as shown. *Fig. F*

Using a ruler, draw a diagonal line on the background square. Stitch ¼in on each side of the drawn line. *Fig. G*

Cut apart directly on the drawn line. *Fig. H*

Press open.

10. Repeat Step 9 with the remaining sewn unit and background square. Press your four completed Flying Geese towards the background fabric. *Fig. I*

Repeat to make a total of sixty (60) 4½in × 8½in large Flying Geese blocks.

11. Repeat Steps 8–10 using the 5¼in print fabric squares and 2⅞in background fabric squares to make a total of sixty (60) 2½in × 4½in small Flying Geese blocks.

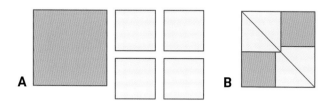

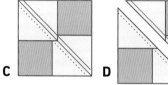

Make four Flying Geese with no waste— what's not to love?

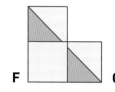

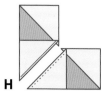

Assembling the Quilt

12. Referring to the quilt layout diagram, lay out all of your pieces into columns. Sew the Flying Geese blocks and the background strips into columns, pressing the seams of alternate columns in opposite directions. Now sew the columns together.

You will have five large Flying Geese blocks left over (one of each colour) once your quilt top is assembled. Head over to Amanda's blog (page 109) to find a cute table runner that'll use them up!

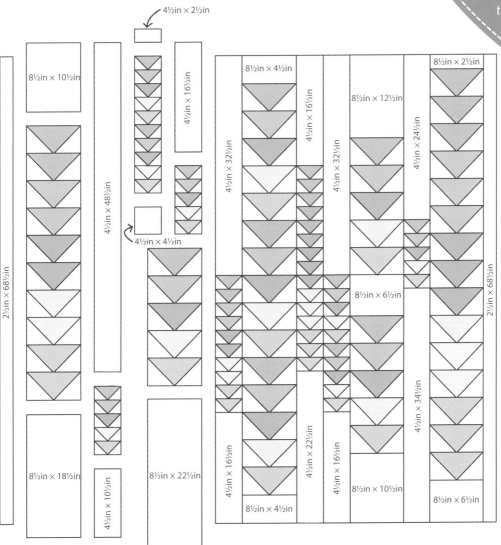

Layout diagram. Mix and match the colour order of your Flying Geese to get a pattern you love.

Quilting and Finishing

13. Cut the backing fabric into two (2) 72in × WOF lengths, remove selvedges and sew together to make a quilt backing roughly 72in × 84in.

14. Make a quilt sandwich with the quilt top, batting and backing.

15. Machine or hand quilt as desired.

16. Sew the seven binding strips together into one long length. Press in half along the length, wrong side together and use this double-fold binding to bind your quilt.

Ooh, just look at those lovely colours!

RAINBOW BRIGHTS

Elizabeth Dackson

Add a pop of colour to your home with this multicoloured mini quilt—made with simple Flying Geese units, it's a quick rainbow make!

QUILT

Finished quilt:
24½in square approx

Such a classic! The Flying Geese unit gets a modern twist in this bright mini quilt.

NOTES

- Seam allowances are ¼in, unless otherwise noted.
- Press all fabrics before cutting.
- Press seams open.
- RST = right sides together
- WOF = width of fabric
- HST = half-square triangle

Mix tones within each colour group to give movement.

Cutting Out

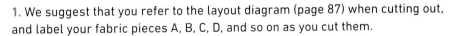

1. We suggest that you refer to the layout diagram (page 87) when cutting out, and label your fabric pieces A, B, C, D, and so on as you cut them.

2. From each group of rainbow fabrics (except light purple and dark purple), cut eight (8) 1½in × 2½in rectangles, for a total of forty-eight (48) rectangles, for Flying Geese units.

3. From the light purple fabric, cut two (2) 3½in squares. Subcut once across the diagonal, for a total of four (4) triangles (for centre unit pieces A10, A11, A12, A13).

Rainbow Brights   **83** ----

4. From the dark purple fabric, cut two (2) 2in squares. Subcut once across the diagonal, for a total of four (4) triangles (for centre unit pieces A2, A3, A4, A5).

5. From the dark grey fabric cut the following:

- Sixteen (16) 1½in squares, for Flying Geese units. Mark a diagonal line on the wrong side of each square.

- Four (4) 1½in squares (A)

- Four (4) 1½in × 4½in rectangles (H)

- Four (4) 1½in × 5½in rectangles (I)

- One (1) 2in square, for accent HSTs

6. From the mid grey fabric cut the following:

- Sixteen (16) 1½in squares, for Flying Geese units. Mark a diagonal line on the wrong side of each square.

- Four (4) 1½in squares (B)

- Four (4) 1½in × 2½in rectangles (C)

- Four (4) 1½in × 3½in rectangles (F)

- Four (4) 1½in × 4½in rectangles (G)

7. From the light grey fabric cut the following:

- Eight (8) 1½in squares, for Flying Geese units. Mark a diagonal line on the wrong side of each square.

- Four (4) 1½in × 2½in rectangles (D)

- Four (4) 1½in × 3½in rectangles (E)

8. From the white fabric cut the following.

- One (1) 2½in square (for centre unit piece A1)

- Two (2) 2½in squares. Subcut across the diagonal once, for a total of four triangles (for centre unit pieces A6, A7, A8, A9).

- Fifty-six (56) 1½in squares, for Flying Geese units. Mark a diagonal line on the wrong side of each square.

- Four (4) 1½in × 5½in rectangles (J)

- Four (4) 1½in × 6½in rectangles (K)

- Four (4) 4½in × 16½in rectangles (L)

- Two (2) 1½in × 3½in rectangles (M)

- Two (2) 3½in × 4½in rectangles (N)

- Two (2) 4½in squares (O)

- One (1) 2in square for accent HSTs. Mark a diagonal line on the wrong side.

9. From the binding fabric cut the following:

- Three (3) 2½in × WOF strips

- Two (2) 6in squares for hanging corners

Paper Piecing the Centre Unit

10. Before you begin, shorten the stitch length on your sewing machine to about 1.5mm. Roughly cut out your copy of Template A, leaving some paper around the outer trim lines.

11. With the template wrong side up, place the A1 white fabric square on top, right side up, and covering the centre square (marked A1). The square will be too big, but this allows for a generous seam allowance and will be trimmed later. Use a dab of washable glue to keep the fabric in place (or pin if you prefer).

12. Now take the A2 dark purple fabric piece and align it right sides together with the A1 fabric piece. Make sure the A2 fabric is hanging approximately ¼in over the seamline where A1 and A2 will be joined. Align the tip of the A2 fabric just over the seam allowance where the A1/A2/A3 fabrics come together. Hold or pin the fabric in place and then sew along the A1/A2 seamline. Sew three or four stitches beyond the seamline marking the A6 and A7 sections, and backstitch to secure.

13. Fold back the paper and trim the excess seam allowance. Set the seam with a hot, dry iron, then unfold the paper and press the fabric open.

14. Repeat this process to add the remaining pieces to the paper template. Once all the pieces are added, press the block well, then trim along the outer dashed line so it is 4½in square. Carefully tear away the foundation paper.

Making the Flying Geese Units

15. For each colour group, you will make a total of eight (8) Flying Geese. The coloured 'geese' will have different neutral 'sky' pieces—see the chart (next page). Begin by taking a blue 1½in × 2½in rectangle, and align a white 1½in square RST with the left side of the rectangle, with the marked line pointing toward the centre of the rectangle. Sew along the line. Trim off the excess seam allowance and press. *Fig. A*

On the opposite side of the rectangle, repeat this process, with a dark grey 1½in square, again with the marked line pointing toward the centre of the rectangle. Press, trim off excess fabric and check that the Flying Geese unit is 1½in × 2½in. Make four units like this in total. *Fig. B*

16. Repeat this process to make four more blue Flying Geese but this time reverse the white and dark grey squares, so the units are mirror images of the first four units. *Fig. C*

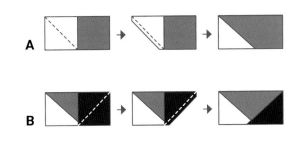

Pay close attention to colour placement.

17. Repeat this process to create all the Flying Geese needed, following the chart below carefully to ensure that you match the neutrals to the correct side of each coloured rectangle. Note that red is the only colour group that has matching right and left sides. You should end up with forty-eight (48) Flying Geese in total.

	Make	Colour group	Right neutral	Left neutral
a	Eight (8)	Red	White	White
b	Four (4)	Orange	White	Dark grey
c	Four (4)	Yellow	White	Mid grey
d	Four (4)	Green	White	Light grey
e	Four (4)	Teal	White	Mid grey
f	Four (4)	Blue	White	Dark grey
g	Four (4)	Orange	Dark grey	White
h	Four (4)	Yellow	Mid grey	White
i	Four (4)	Green	Light grey	White
j	Four (4)	Teal	Mid grey	White
k	Four (4)	Blue	Dark grey	White

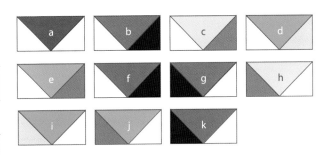

Making the Accent HSTs

18. To create the two accent half-square triangles, take the 2in marked white square and place it RST with the 2in dark grey square, with the marked white square facing you. Pin as needed. Sew a scant ¼in parallel to either side of the marked line. Cut the unit apart on the marked line. Press the seams of the two half-square triangle units open. Trim each unit down to 1½in square, keeping the seam along the diagonal.

TIP: BLOC LOC RULER
Have you ever used a Bloc Loc ruler? These rulers have a special groove for lining up the seam of a half-square triangle unit at a 45-degree angle, which makes trimming a breeze.

Building the Quilt

19. You now have all the units you need to build the quilt top. As you can see in the layout diagram, the Flying Geese units are sewn together in mirror image colour pairs and then joined together with specific grey squares and rectangles to make border strips. Once joined, the strips are added to the sides of the quilt first, and then the top and bottom.

20. For the first border, take two mirror image blue Flying Geese units and sew them together. *Fig. D*

Make two units like this. Take two more mirror image blue Flying Geese units, sew them together and then add a 1½in dark grey square (piece A) to either end. *Fig. E*

Make two units like this.

21. Sew the paired blue Flying Geese units to the sides of the central unit, pressing seams outwards. Then add the longer units to the top and bottom of the central unit and press seams outwards. *Fig. F*

22. Build up the other Flying Geese border strips using the same process. Note that from border two onwards, each of the pairs of Flying Geese at the sides of the quilt will need squares or rectangles added before joining the strips to the quilt. The illustration shows the second border piecing. Make sure that you use the correct colours (especially the greys), following the colours and letter order shown in the layout diagram. When you have added the red Flying Geese border your quilt top should be 16½in square. *Fig. G*

Adding the Outer Border

23. The outer border has two pieced corners, with accent HSTs. Take the white/dark grey HSTs made earlier and sew a white M rectangle to the top of one HST and the bottom of the other HST. Press seams towards the dark fabric. Now take the white N rectangles and sew one to the left-hand side of the unit, and the other to the right-hand side.

These two corner units should now be 4½in square.

24. Take two of the white L rectangles and sew them to the sides of the quilt. Press seams outwards. Create the top border by sewing the top left corner unit to a white L rectangle. Sew a white square O

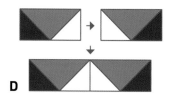

D

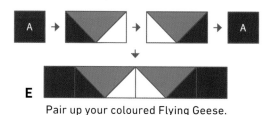

E

Pair up your coloured Flying Geese.

F

Add each new colour in rounds, following the layout diagram for placement of the neutral fabrics in each border.

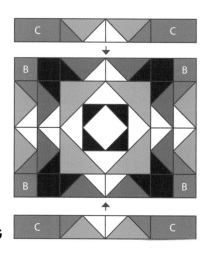

G

to the right-hand side. Repeat for the lower border but reversing the position of square O and the corner unit. Now sew these two units to the top and bottom of the quilt to finish the quilt top.

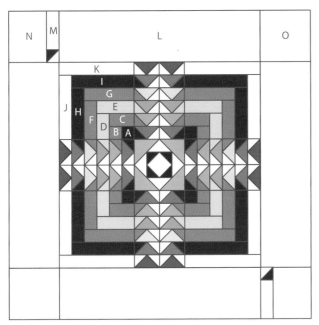

Layout diagram

Quilting and Finishing

25. Make a quilt sandwich by laying the backing fabric right side down, the batting and the quilt top right side up. Baste with pins or spray adhesive, as preferred. Quilt as desired. Our quilt was free-motion machine quilted in an all-over vermicelli pattern.

26. Trim off excess batting and backing fabric and square up the quilt. Tidy any thread ends. Sew the binding strips together with 45-degree seams and press the seams open. Fold the binding in half along the length, wrong sides together, and press.

27. Before attaching binding, press the two 6in binding squares in half, wrong sides together. This creates hanging corners for the quilt. Pin the hanging corners in the top right and left corners of the back side of the quilt. Once the corners are pinned in place, machine the binding to the front side of the quilt as normal, thus attaching the corners in place securely. Hand stitch the binding to the back of the quilt to finish. Feel free to use a Sharpie or other marker pen on the hanging corners to label your mini quilt!

Don't be afraid of white space—those big borders and matching binding make the colours really pop!

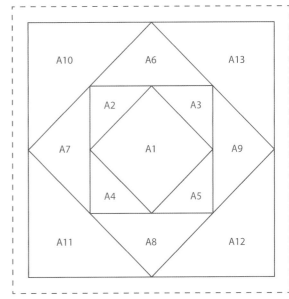

Template A: Enlarge 150%.

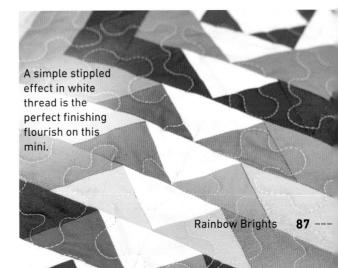

A simple stippled effect in white thread is the perfect finishing flourish on this mini.

SPACE BLOSSOM

Nicole Calver

Brighten up cold winter days with eye-catching colour combos and high-contrast piecing.

QUILT

Finished quilt:
72in × 92in approx

Fabrics used: Solid fabrics are from the Lawn collection by Cotton + Steel.

You Will Need

Background fabric (white):
5¼yds

Teal fabric: 1yd

Pink fabric: 1yd

Red fabric: 1¼yds

Navy print fabric: 4¼yds

Yellow fabric: ⅜yd

Backing fabric: 5½yds

Batting: 78in × 98in

Binding fabric: ¾yd

NOTES

• Seam allowances are ¼in, unless otherwise noted.

• Press all seams open.

• HST = half-square triangles

• FG = Flying Geese

• RST = right sides together

• WOF = width of fabric

• WST = wrong sides together

Simple HST and Flying Geese units combine to make this visually striking pattern.

Cutting Out

1. From the background fabric cut:

• Nine (9) 3½in × WOF strips. Subcut to give one hundred (100) 3½in squares.

• Five (5) 3⅞in × WOF strips. Subcut to give forty-four (44) 3⅞in squares.

• Three (3) 6½in × WOF strips. Subcut to give sixteen (16) 6½in squares.

• One (1) 7¼in × WOF strip. Subcut to give four (4) 7¼in squares.

• Thirteen (13) 8in × WOF strips. Subcut to give sixty-one (61) 8in squares.

2. From the teal fabric cut:

• One (1) 3⅞in × WOF strip. Subcut to give eight (8) 3⅞in squares.

• Eight (8) 3½in × WOF strips. Subcut three (3) of the strips to give thirty-two (32) 3½in squares. Subcut three (3) of the strips to give sixteen (16) 3½in × 6½in rectangles.

3. From the pink fabric cut:

- One (1) 3⅞in × WOF strip. Subcut to give eight (8) 3⅞in squares.

- Six (6) 3½in × WOF strips. Subcut three (3) of the strips to give thirty-two (32) 3½in squares. Subcut three (3) of the strips to give six-teen (16) 3½in × 6½in rectangles.

- Two (2) 1½in × WOF strips.

4. From the red fabric cut:

- Two (2) 6½in × WOF strips. Subcut to give twelve (12) 6½in squares.

- Two (2) 12½in × WOF strips. Subcut one (1) strip to give three (3) 12½in squares. Subcut the re-maining strip to give one (1) 12½in square and four (4) 6½in squares.

- Two (2) 1½in × WOF strips.

5. From the navy print cut:

- Two (2) 6½in × WOF strips. Subcut to give twelve (12) 6½in squares.

- Three (3) 7¼in × WOF strips. Subcut to give eleven (11) 7¼in squares.

- Thirteen (13) 8in × WOF strips. Subcut to give sixty-one (61) 8in squares.

- Two (2) 2½in × WOF strips.

- Two (2) 5½in × WOF strips.

6. From the yellow fabric cut one (1) 6½in square and three (3) 1½in × WOF strips.

7. From the binding fabric cut nine (9) 2¼in × WOF strips.

Piecing the HST Units

8. Take one 8in background square and on the wrong side mark a diagonal line from corner to corner. Take one 8in navy square and place the squares RST with the marked

square on top. Sew ¼in each side of both diagonal lines.

9. Cut the square in half both horizontally and vertically to give four smaller squares.

10. Cut each of the smaller squares apart along the marked line. *Fig. A*

11. Open out each square and press. Keeping the 45-degree line of your ruler aligned with the diagonal seam, trim each unit to 3½in square. *Fig. B*

You will now have eight identical navy/background HSTs.

12. Repeat Steps 8–11 with the remaining 8in background and 8in navy squares to make a total of two hundred and forty-four navy/background HSTs.

Piecing the FG Units

13. Take one 7¼in background square and four 3⅞in teal squares. On the wrong side of each teal square mark a diagonal line from corner to corner.

14. RST place a teal square on op-posite corners of the background square—they will overlap in the centre. Sew ¼in each side of the diagonal line from corner to corner of the background square. *Fig. C*

15. Cut apart along the marked line to make two units, then press the units open.

16. Take one of the units from Step 15 and, RST, place one of the remaining 3⅞in teal squares on the corner of the unit. Sew ¼in each side of the marked line. *Fig. D*

17. Cut apart along the marked line to make two FG units. Press the units open. Trim to 6½in × 3½in. *Fig. E*

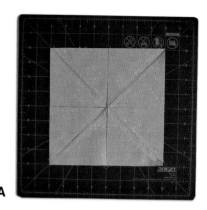

A

B

C

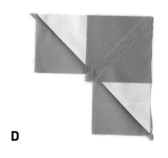

D

E

18. Repeat Steps 16 and 17 with the remaining unit from Step 15 and the remaining 3⅞in teal square to make a total of four teal/background FG units.

19. Repeat Steps 13–18 to make a total of eight teal/background FG units, eight pink/background FG units and forty-four background/navy FG units.

Piecing the Square-in-Square Units

20. Take one 6½in red square and four 3½in teal squares. On the wrong side of each teal square mark a diagonal line from corner to corner.

21. RST, place a teal square on opposite corners of the red square with the marked lines running from outer edge to outer edge of the red square.

22. Sew on the marked line and trim ¼in beyond the stitched line. *Fig. F*

Flip the corner open and press. *Fig. G*

23. Repeat Steps 21 and 22 on the two remaining corners with the two remaining teal squares to complete one 6½in red/teal square-in-square unit. *Fig. H*

24. Repeat Steps 20–23 to make a total of eight 6½in red/teal square-in-square units.

25. Repeat Steps 20–23 with the remaining eight 6½in red squares and thirty-two 3½in pink squares to make eight 6½in red/pink square-in-square units.

26. Repeat Steps 20–23 with four 12½in red squares and sixteen 6½in background squares to make four 12½in red/background square-in-square units.

27. Repeat Steps 20–23 with the 6½in yellow square and four 3½in background squares to make one 6½in yellow/background square-in-square unit.

28. Repeat Steps 20–23 with the twelve 6½in navy squares and forty-eight 3½in background squares make twelve 6½in navy/background square-in-square units.

Piecing the Corner-Square Triangle Units

29. Take one 3½in × 6½in teal rectangle and one 3½in background square. On the wrong side of the background square mark a diagonal line from corner to corner.

30. RST, place the background square on top of the teal rectangle with the marked line running from top left to bottom right. *Fig. I*

31. Sew on the marked line and trim ¼in beyond the stitched line. *Fig. J*

Flip the corner open and press.

32. Repeat Steps 29–31 with the marked line running from the top right to bottom left. You will now have one pair of teal/background corner-square triangle units. *Fig. K*

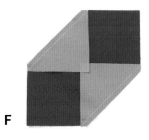
F

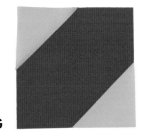
G

H

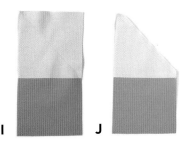
I   J

K

33. Repeat Steps 29–32 to make a total of eight pairs of teal/background corner-square triangle units.

34. Repeat Steps 29–32 with the 3½in × 6½in pink rectangles to make a total of eight pairs of pink/background corner-square triangle units.

Assembling the Blocks

35. Take eight navy/background HSTs and one 3½in background square. Arrange in a three-by-three layout as shown. *Fig. L*

36. Join the pieces into rows and then join the rows to complete one nine-patch unit. Repeat to make a total of four nine-patch units.

37. Take one teal/background FG unit and two navy/background HSTs. Join the pieces as shown. *Fig. M*

38. Take one 6½in red/teal square-in-square unit and one pair of teal/background corner-square triangle units. Join the pieces as shown. *Fig. N*

39. Join the unit made in Step 37 to the top of the unit made in Step 38 as shown to complete one blossom unit. *Fig. O*

40. Repeat Steps 37–39 to make a total of four blossom units.

41. Take the four nine-patch units, the four blossom units and one 12½in red/background square-in-square unit. Arrange into three rows of three units each as shown. *Fig. P*

Join into rows and then join the rows to complete one teal block.

42. Repeat Steps 35–41 to make a second teal block.

43. Repeat Steps 35–41 with the pink/background FG units, the 6½in red/pink square-in-square units and pairs of pink/background corner-square triangle units to make two pink blocks.

L

M

N

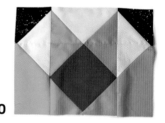

O

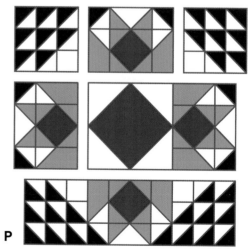

P

Make sure you orientate the blocks correctly to make the star design.

Edging the Blocks

44. Take ten background/navy HSTs and join as shown to make one edging strip. *Fig. Q*

Repeat to make a total of eight strips.

45. Take one teal block, two edging strips and one background/navy HST and arrange as shown. *Fig. R*

Join an edging strip to the right-hand side of the block. Join the HST to the right-hand edge of the top edging strip and then join this to the top of the block.

46. Repeat Step 45 to edge the second teal block.

47. Repeat Steps 45 and 46 with the two pink blocks, this time adding the side edging strip to the left-hand side of the blocks.

Assembling the Quilt Top

48. Take eleven background/navy FG units and join into a row, making sure that they're all pointing in the same direction. Repeat to make a total of four FG unit strips.

49. Arrange the blocks into a two-by-two layout with a teal block at the top right and bottom left and a pink block at the top left and bottom right.

50. Join the top and bottom blocks into pairs with an FG unit strip between them, with the FG units pointing towards the centre of the quilt.

51. Join a FG unit strip to each side of the 6½in yellow/background square-in-square unit, with the FG units pointing towards the centre. Join the top and bottom pairs of blocks to each side of this pieced strip to complete the quilt centre.

52. Take the following:

- Two 3½in × WOF teal strips
- Two 1½in × WOF pink strips
- Two 1½in × WOF red strips
- Two 2½in × WOF navy strips
- Two 5½in × WOF navy strips
- Two 1½in × WOF yellow strips

Join the strips into pairs end-to-end with a straight seam, then trim to 72½in.

53. Take the 6½in navy/background square-in-square units and join into a row, measuring 72½in wide.

54. To make the top border join the following, from top to bottom:

- One 2½in × 72½in navy strip
- One 1½in × 72½in pink strip
- One 1½in × 72½in red strip
- One navy/background square-in-square row
- One 1½in × 72½in yellow strip

Join this section to the top of the quilt centre.

55. To make the bottom border join the following, from top to bottom:

- One 1½in × 72½in yellow strip
- One 5½in × 72½in navy strip
- One 3½in × 72½in teal strip

Join this section to the bottom of the quilt centre to complete the quilt top.

Q

R

Layout diagram

Quilting and Finishing

56. Cut the backing fabric in half across the width. Remove the selvedges and then re-join the pieces along the length with a ½in seam. Press the seam open.

57. Press the quilt top and backing well. Make a quilt sandwich by placing the backing fabric right side down, the batting on top, then the quilt top centrally and right side up. The backing and batting are slightly larger than the quilt top. Baste the layers together using your preferred method.

58. Quilt as desired. Nicole hand quilted echoing shapes within each block.

59. Trim off the excess batting and backing fabric and square up the quilt.

60. Take the 2¼in × WOF strips and join end-to-end using diagonal seams. Press the seams open and trim away the dog-ears. Fold in half lengthwise, WST, and press.

61. Sew the binding to the right side of the quilt, folding a mitre at each corner.

62. Fold the binding over to the back of the quilt and hand stitch in place to finish.

Minimalist quilting is ideal for this high-impact quilt.

Pieced sashing is a lovely way to finish off a quilt and add more colour to the design.

ALL AROUND ARROWS
Julie Rutter

Go bold with mix 'n' match print units to make graphic rounds of arrows of all different shapes and sizes.

MAKE A MATCH
The springtime shades in this quilt pack a punch, but you can choose colours to suit your home's style.

QUILT

Finished quilt:
57in square approx

Fabrics used: Print fabrics are from the Blueberry Park collection by Karen Lewis for Robert Kaufman Fabrics in the following prints. Fabric A: Ocean. Fabric B: Pond. Fabric C: Hibiscus. Fabric D: Ultramarine. Fabric E: Pool. Fabric F: Limelight. Fabric G: Cypress. Fabric H: Zucchini. Fabric I: Stratos. Fabric J: Ice Frappe. Background fabric: Snow. The backing fabric is Pacific from the Widescreen collection by Carolyn Friedlander for Robert Kaufman Fabrics.

You Will Need

Print fabrics A–J: ½yd each of ten (10) different prints

Background fabric: 3½yds

Backing fabric: 3½yds

Batting: 63in square

Binding: ⅝yd

NOTES

• Seam allowances are ¼in, unless otherwise noted.

• Press seams open, unless otherwise instructed.

• Print fabric requirements are generous to allow for mixing and matching of colour combos. If the pattern is followed exactly, you will have leftover fabric.

• HST = half-square triangle

• HRT = half-rectangle triangle

• RST = right sides together

• WOF = width of fabric

• WST = wrong sides together

Cutting Out

1. From Fabric A cut:

• Two (2) 10in × 5¼in

• Two (2) 10½in × 5¾in

• One (1) 19½in × 4½in

• One (1) 2½in × 10in

2. From Fabric B cut two (2) 5¼in squares and four (4) 10½in × 5¾in.

3. From Fabric C cut:

• Two (2) 10in × 5¼in

• Two (2) 10½in × 5¾in

• One (1) 2½in × 14¾in

• One (1) 2½in × 5¼in

• One (1) 1½in square

• One (1) 4¼in × 2½in

• One (1) 2½in × 14¾in

Combine basic quilting units to make a variety of complex-looking arrow-shaped blocks.

4. From Fabric D cut:

- Three (3) 10in × 5¼in
- Two (2) 5¼in squares
- One (1) 19½in × 4½in

5. From Fabric E cut:

- Two (2) 5¾in squares
- One (1) 10in × 5¼in
- Two (2) 10½in × 5¾in
- One (1) 1½in square
- One (1) 5¼in square
- One (1) 4¼in × 2½in

6. From Fabric F cut:

- Two (2) 10in × 5¼in
- Four (4) 5¼in squares
- Two (2) 5¾in × 4¾in
- Two (2) 2½in × 5¼in
- One (1) 1½in square
- One (1) 2½in × 4¼in
- One (1) 2½in × 5¼in

7. From Fabric G cut:

- Two (2) 5¾in squares
- One (1) 10in × 5¼in
- Two (2) 5¼in squares
- Two (2) 10½in × 5¾in
- One (1) 14¾in × 2½in

8. From Fabric H cut:

- Two (2) 5¾in squares
- Two (2) 5¼in squares
- Two (2) 10½in × 5¾in

9. From Fabric I cut four (4) 5¾in × 4¾in and two (2) 10½in × 5¾in.

10. From Fabric J cut:

- Two (2) 5¾in squares
- One (1) 10in × 5¼in

- Two (2) 5¼in squares
- One (1) 1½in square
- One (1) 2½in × 4¼in

11. From the background fabric cut:

- Eight (8) 5¾in squares
- Twenty-four (24) 5¼in squares
- Seven (7) 10in × 5¼in
- Six (6) 5¾in × 4¾in
- Sixteen (16) 10½in × 5¾in
- Four (4) 19½in × 3¼in
- Four (4) 14¾in × 4¼in
- Two (2) 4¼in × 10in
- Six (6) 4¼in × 5¼in
- Four (4) 4¼in squares
- Six (6) 5¼in squares

12. From the binding fabric, cut six (6) 2½in × WOF strips.

Piecing the Half-Square Triangle Units

13. Take one Fabric E 5¾in square and one background 5¾in square. On the wrong side of the background square mark a diagonal line from corner to corner. Place the squares RST, with the marked square on top, then stitch ¼in either side of the marked line. *Fig. A*

14. Cut through both layers on the marked line. *Fig. B*

Open the units out and press. Trim to 5¼in square. You will now have two Fabric E half-square triangle units. *Fig. C*

15. Repeat Steps 13 and 14 with the remaining 5¾in squares to make the following HST units:

- Four (4) Fabric E HST units— you need three for this quilt, so discard one.
- Four (4) Fabric G HST units— you need three for this quilt, so discard one.
- Four (4) Fabric H HST units
- Four (4) Fabric J HST units— you need three for this quilt, so discard one.

Piecing the Flying Geese Units

16. Take one Fabric A 10in × 5¼in rectangle and two background 5¼in squares. On the wrong side of each square mark a diagonal line from corner to corner.

17. Place one square RST with the Fabric A rectangle, with the marked line running from the bottom corner of the rectangle to the top middle edge, as shown. Stitch along the marked line.

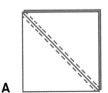

A

B

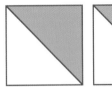

C

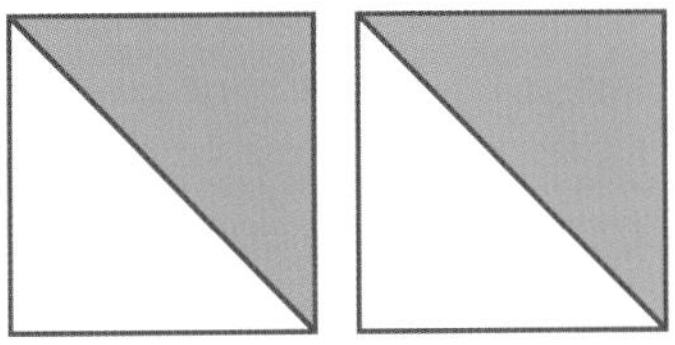

18. Trim to a ¼in seam allowance, as shown. *Fig. D*

Open the unit out and press.

19. Repeat Steps 17 and 18 for the other corner, using the remaining background fabric square. Trim to 10in × 5¼in. You will now have one Fabric A Flying Geese unit. *Fig. E*

20. Repeat Steps 16–19 with the remaining 10in × 5¼in rectangles and background fabric 5¼in squares to make the following Flying Geese units:

- Two (2) Fabric A Flying Geese units
- Two (2) Fabric C Flying Geese units
- Three (3) Fabric D Flying Geese units
- One (1) Fabric E Flying Geese unit
- Two (2) Fabric F Flying Geese units
- One (1) Fabric G Flying Geese unit
- One (1) Fabric J Flying Geese unit

21. Take one background 10in × 5¼in rectangle and two Fabric B 5¼in squares. Repeat Steps 16–19 to make one Fabric B Flying Geese unit.

22. Repeat Step 21 with the remaining background fabric 10in × 5¼in rectangles and 5¼in squares to make the following Flying Geese units:

- Two (2) Fabric A Flying Geese units
- One (1) Fabric D Flying Geese unit
- Two (2) Fabric F Flying Geese units
- One (1) Fabric G Flying Geese unit
- One (1) Fabric H Flying Geese unit
- One (1) Fabric J Flying Geese unit

Piecing the Half-Rectangle Triangle Units

23. Take one Fabric F 5¾in × 4¾in rectangle and one background 5¾in × 4¾in rectangle.

24. Place the Fabric F rectangle right side up with the long edges at the top and bottom, then measure and mark ½in from the top left and bottom right corners, as shown. *Fig. F*

25. Place the background rectangle wrong side up, then measure and mark ½in from the top right and bottom left corners. *Fig. G*

Mark a diagonal line between the two marked points.

26. Place the rectangles RST with the background rectangle on top and matching up the ½in marks. *Fig. H*

Stitch ¼in either side of marked line and then cut through both layers on the marked line. *Fig. I*

27. Open the units out and press. Trim to 5¼in × 4¼in, with the seam running from corner to corner, to make two Fabric F half-rectangle triangle units. *Fig. J*

You need one for this quilt, so discard one.

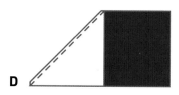

D

E

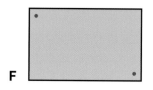

F

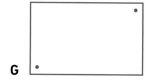

G

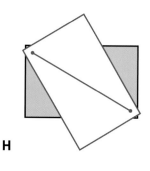

H

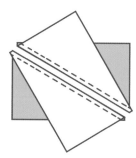

I

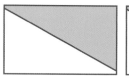

J

28. Take two Fabric I 5¾in × 4¾in rectangles and two background 5¾in × 4¾in rectangles. Repeat Steps 23–27 to make a total of four Fabric I HRT units. You need three for this quilt, so discard one.

29. Take one Fabric F 5¾in × 4¾in rectangle and one background 5¾in × 4¾in rectangle.

30. Place the Fabric F rectangle right side up with the long edges at the top and bottom, then measure and mark ½in from the top right and bottom left corners.

31. Place the background rectangle wrong side up, then measure and mark ½in from the top left and bottom right corners. Mark a diagonal line between the two marked points.

32. Place the two rectangles RST with the background rectangle on top and matching up the ½in marks. Stitch ¼in either side of marked line and then cut through both layers on the marked line.

33. Open the units out and press. Trim to 5¼in × 4¼in, with the seam running from corner to corner, to make two Fabric F HRT units. You need one for this quilt, so discard one.

34. Take two Fabric I 5¾in × 4¾in rectangles and two background 5¾in × 4¾in rectangles. Repeat Steps 30–33 to make a total of four Fabric I HRT units. You need three for this quilt, so discard one.

35. Take one Fabric A 10½in × 5¾in rectangle and one background 10½in × 5¾in rectangle. Repeat Steps 24–27, this time trimming to 10in × 5¼in, to make two Fabric A HRTs. You need one for this quilt, so discard one.

36. Repeat Step 35 to make the following HRT units:

- Four (4) Fabric B HRT units— you need three for this quilt, so discard one.

- Two (2) Fabric C HRT units— you need one for this quilt, so discard one.

- Two (2) Fabric E HRT units— you need one for this quilt, so discard one.

- Two (2) Fabric G HRT units— you need one for this quilt, so discard one.

- Two (2) Fabric H HRT units— you need one for this quilt, so discard one.

- Two (2) Fabric I HRT units— you need one for this quilt, so discard one.

37. Take one Fabric A 10½in × 5¾in rectangle and one background 10½in × 5¾in background rectangle. Repeat Steps 30–33, this time trimming to 10in × 5¼in, to make two Fabric A HRT units. You need one for this quilt, so discard one.

38. Repeat Step 37 to make the following HRT units:

- Four (4) Fabric B HRT units— you need three for this quilt, so discard one.

- Two (2) Fabric C HRT units— you need one for this quilt, so discard one.

- Two (2) Fabric E HRT units— you need one for this quilt, so discard one.

- Two (2) Fabric G HRT units— you need one for this quilt, so discard one.

- Two (2) Fabric H HRT units— you need one for this quilt, so discard one.

- Two (2) Fabric I HRT units— you need one for this quilt, so discard one.

Piecing Unit A

39. Take the Fabric A 19½in × 4½in rectangle and two background 19½in × 3¼in rectangles. Sew one background rectangle to each long edge to complete one Fabric A Unit A.

40. Repeat Step 39 with the Fabric D 19½in × 4½in rectangle to make one Fabric D Unit A.

Piecing Unit B

41. Take the Fabric C 2½in × 14¾in rectangle and sew a background 4¼in × 14¾in rectangle to each long edge to complete one Fabric C Unit B.

42. Repeat Step 41 with the Fabric G 2½in × 14¾in rectangle to make one Fabric G Unit B.

Piecing Unit C

43. Take the Fabric A 2½in × 10in rectangle and sew a background 4¼in × 10in rectangle to each long edge to complete Unit C.

Piecing Unit D

44. Take the Fabric C 2½in × 5¼in rectangle and sew a background 4¼in × 5¼in rectangle to each long edge to complete one Fabric C Unit D.

45. Repeat Step 44 with the two Fabric F 2½in × 5¼in rectangles to make a total of two of Fabric F Unit D.

Piecing the Blocks

46. Block 1: Take three Fabric J HST units and one 5¼in background square. Join into a four-patch unit. *Fig. K*

47. Block 2: Take two Fabric F Flying Geese units. Join on their long edges. *Fig. L*

48. Block 3: Take two Fabric E 10in × 5¾in HRT units. Join on the Fabric E long edge. *Fig. M*

49. Block 4: Take one Fabric G Flying Geese unit and one Fabric G Unit B. Join the FG unit to one short edge of Unit B, as shown. *Fig. N*

50. Block 5: Take two Fabric H 10in × 5¾in HRT units. Join on the Fabric H long edge. *Fig. O*

51. Block 6: Take two Fabric I 10in × 5¾in HRT units. Join on the Fabric I long edge. *Fig. P*

K
Block 1

L
Block 2

M
Block 3

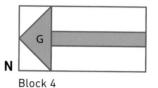
N
Block 4

O
Block 5

P
Block 6

52. Block 7: Take one Fabric D Unit A and two Fabric D Flying Geese. Join the two FG units on the long edge, then join to the right-hand side of Unit A. *Fig. Q*

53. Block 8: Take two Fabric A 10in × 5¾in HRT units. Join on the Fabric A long edge. *Fig. R*

54. Block 9: Take one Fabric C Flying Geese unit and one Fabric C Unit B. Join the FG unit to one short edge of Unit B, as shown. *Fig. S*

55. Block 10: Take two Fabric C 10in × 5¾in HRT units. Join on one long edge. *Fig. T*

56. Block 11: Take the following units:

- One (1) Fabric A Flying Geese unit
- One (1) Fabric A Unit C
- Two (2) Fabric G HST units

Join the Fabric A edge of the FG unit to one short edge of Unit C. Join the two HSTs along the Fabric G edge and then join them to the other short edge of Unit C, as shown. *Fig. U*

57. Block 12: Take the following units:

- One (1) Fabric C 1½in square
- One (1) Fabric E 1½in square
- One (1) Fabric F 1½in square
- One (1) Fabric J 1½in square
- One (1) Fabric C 4¼in × 2½in
- One (1) Fabric E 4¼in × 2½in
- One (1) Fabric F 2½in × 4¼in
- One (1) Fabric J 2½in × 4¼in
- Four (4) background 4¼in squares

Arrange them as shown. Join the units into rows and then join the rows.

Q
Block 7

R
Block 8

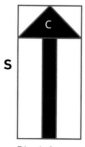
S
Block 9

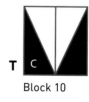
T
Block 10

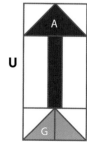
U
Block 11

58. Block 12 (continued): Take the following units:

- One (1) Fabric C Flying Geese unit
- One (1) Fabric E Unit B Flying Geese unit
- One (1) Fabric F Unit B Flying Geese unit
- One (1) Fabric J Unit B Flying Geese unit
- Four (4) 5¼in background squares

Arrange them as shown with the unit from Step 57. Join the units into rows and then join the rows. *Fig. V*

59. Block 13: Take two Fabric B 10in × 5¾in HRT units. Join on the background fabric long edge. *Fig. W*

60. Block 14: Take two Fabric B 10in × 5¾in HRT units. Join on the Fabric B long edge. *Fig. X*

61. Block 15: Take the following units:

- One (1) Fabric F Unit D
- Two (2) Fabric F 5¼in × 4¼in HRT units
- One (1) Fabric F 2½in × 5¼in rectangle

Join the two HRT units to each long side of the Fabric F rectangle, as shown. Join to a long edge of Unit H. *Fig. Y*

62. Block 16: Take one Fabric F Unit H and one Fabric F Flying Geese unit. Join on their long edges. *Fig. Z*

63. Block 17: Take one Fabric G HST unit and one 5¼in background square. Join the HST to the background square. *Fig. AA*

V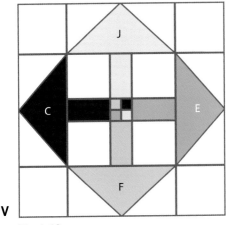
Block 12

W
Block 13

X
Block 14

Y
Block 15

Z
Block 16

AA
Block 17

BB
Block 18

64. Block 18: Take one Fabric A Flying Geese unit and one Fabric A Unit A. Join the FG unit to a short edge of Unit E. *Fig. BB*

65. Block 19: Take four Fabric H HST units. Arrange as shown and join them into pairs. Join the pairs. *Fig. CC*

66. Block 20: Take the following units:

- One (1) Fabric C Unit D
- One (1) 2½in × 14¾in Fabric C rectangle
- Six (6) Fabric I 5¼in × 4¼in HRT units

Join the HRT units into two columns, as shown. Sew the columns to either side of the Fabric C rectangle. Join Unit D to the bottom edge. *Fig. DD*

CC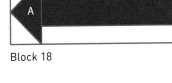
Block 19

DD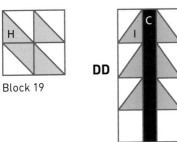
Block 20

67. Block 21: Take three Fabric E HSTs and one Fabric E 5¼in square. Join into a four-patch unit, as shown. *Fig. EE*

68. Block 22: Take two Fabric B 10in × 5¾in HRT units. Join on one long edge. *Fig. FF*

69. Block 23: Take one Fabric G Flying Geese unit and one Fabric J Flying Geese unit. Join on their long edges. *Fig. GG*

70. Block 24: Take one Fabric B Flying Geese unit and one Fabric H Flying Geese unit. Join on their long edges. *Fig. HH*

71. Block 25: Take two Fabric G 10in × 5¾in HRT units. Join on one long edge. *Fig. II*

72. Block 26: Take two Fabric D Flying Geese. Join on their long edges. *Fig. JJ*

73. Arrange the blocks into rows, referring to the layout diagram for placement. Join the blocks into rows, then join the rows to complete the quilt top, which should measure 57½in square.

Quilting and Finishing

74. Press the quilt top well. Make a quilt sandwich with the backing fabric, batting and quilt top. Baste the layers together using your preferred method.

75. Quilt as desired. Julie quilted an improv square spiral from the centre.

76. Trim off excess batting and backing fabric and square up the quilt.

77. Join the binding strips together end-to-end using

EE 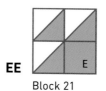 FF 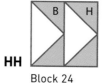 GG

Block 21 Block 22 Block 23

HH II JJ

Block 24 Block 25 Block 26

The big blocks are perfect for showing off intricate prints.

diagonal seams. Press the seams open and trim away the dog-ears. Fold in half lengthwise, WST, and press.

78. Sew the binding to the front of the quilt, folding a mitre at each corner, then fold the binding over to the back of the quilt and hand stitch in place to finish.

Layout diagram

LOOKING UP
Nicole Calver

Combine monochrome prints with soft blues and a pink colour pop to stitch up supersize arrows using Flying Geese units.

COLOUR COMBOS
The bold black and white prints are all by Cotton + Steel. Add a pop of bright pink to highlight the design.

QUILT

Finished quilt:
72in × 96in

Fabrics used: Monochrome print fabrics are from the Black & White collection by Cotton + Steel.

You Will Need

Black prints: ½yd each of six (6) different prints

Neutral prints: ⅝yd each of eight (8) different prints

Blue prints: ½yd each of eight (8) different prints

Pink print: One (1) fat quarter

Backing fabric: 6yds

Batting: 76in × 100in

Binding fabric: ¾yd

NOTES

• Seam allowances are ¼in, unless otherwise noted.

• Press seams open, unless otherwise instructed.

• FG = Flying Geese

• RST = right sides together

• WOF = width of fabric

• WST = wrong sides together

• Fabric and Sulky Threads provided by Cotton + Steel (cottonandsteelfabrics.com)

Cutting Out

1. From each of the black print fabrics cut two (2) 8½in × WOF strips. Subcut each strip into two (2) 8½in squares and two (2) 6½in × 12½in rectangles. You will only need a total of twenty-three of each, so will have one of each left over.

2. From each of four of the neutral print fabrics cut:

• Two (2) 6½in × WOF strips. Subcut each strip into three (3) 6½in × 12½in rectangles.

• Two (2) 2½in × WOF strips. Subcut each strip into three (3) 2½in × 8½in rectangles.

The arrows in this quilt are a great way to show off prints from your fave collection.

3. From each of the remaining four neutral print fabrics cut:

- Two (2) 2⅞in × WOF strips. Subcut each strip into fourteen (14) 2⅞in squares.

- Two (2) 6½in × WOF strips. Subcut each strip into six (6) 6½in squares and one (1) 2⅞in square.

4. From each of the blue print fabrics, cut:

- One (1) 6½in × WOF strip. Subcut each strip into six (6) 6½in square.

- One (1) 2½in × WOF strip. Subcut each strip into three (3) 2½in × 12½in rectangles.

5. From three of the blue print fabrics also cut one (1) 5¼in × WOF strip. Subcut each strip into eight (8) 5¼in squares.

6. From the pink print fabric cut:

- One (1) 8½in square

- One (1) 6½in × 12½in rectangle

- Six (6) 5¼in squares

7. From the binding fabric, cut nine (9) 2½in strips.

Making the Small FG Units

8. Take four of the 2⅞in neutral print squares. On the wrong side of each square, mark a diagonal line from corner to corner.

9. Take one 5¼in blue print square and, RST, place a neutral print square on two opposite corners, with the marked lines running from corner to corner of the blue print square. The neutral print squares will overlap in the centre. *Fig. A*

10. Sew ¼in either side of the marked lines, then cut the unit apart on the lines. *Fig. B*

Press the two units open. *Fig. C*

11. RST, place a neutral print square on the remaining blue print corner of each of the units from Step 10, with the marked line running towards the centre. *Fig. D*

12. Sew ¼in either side of the marked line, then cut the units apart on the line. *Fig. E*

Press the two units open to complete four blue/neutral Small FG units. *Fig. F*

13. Repeat Steps 8–12 with the remaining 5¼in blue print squares to make a total of ninety-six (96) blue/neutral Small FG units.

14. Repeat Steps 8–12 with the 5¼in pink print squares to make a total of twenty-four (24) pink/neutral Small FG units.

A

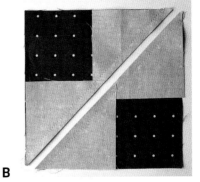

B

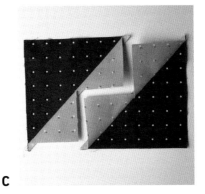

C

D

E

F

Making the Large FG Units

15. Take two of the 6½in neutral print squares. On the wrong side of each square, mark a diagonal line from corner to corner.

16. Take one 6½in × 12½in black print rectangle. RST, place one 6½in neutral print square on one corner of the rectangle, with the diagonal line running from the bottom corner to the centre of the top edge. *Fig. G*

17. Stitch on the marked line and then trim ¼in beyond the stitched line. *Fig. H*

Flip the corner open and press the seam towards the neutral triangle. *Fig. I*

Nicole stitched on either side of her line to make an extra HST to use in another project.

18. Repeat Steps 16 and 17 with the other corner of the black print rectangle to complete one black/neutral Large FG unit. *Fig. J*

19. Repeat Steps 15–18 to make a total of twenty-three black/neutral Large FG units.

20. Repeat Steps 15–18 with the blue 6½in squares and the neutral print 6½in × 12½in rectangles to make a total of twenty-four neutral/blue Large FG units.

21. Repeat Steps 15–18 with the neutral print 6½in squares and pink print 6½in × 12½in rectangle to make one pink/neutral Large FG unit.

Piecing Block A

22. Take one black/neutral Large FG unit and one neutral/blue Large FG unit. Join them as shown, with both units pointing up, to make one black Block A. *Fig. K*

23. Repeat Step 22 to make a total of twenty-three of black Block A.

24. Repeat Step 22 with one neutral/blue Large FG unit and one pink/neutral Large FG unit to make one pink Block A, with the pink unit at the bottom.

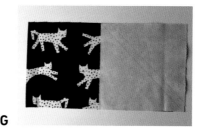

G

J

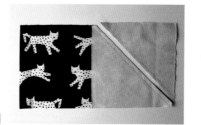

H

I

K

Piecing Block B

25. Take three blue/neutral Small FG units and one pink/neutral Small FG unit. Join them as shown, with all the units pointing left. *Fig. L*

26. Take one black print 8½in square. Join it to the top of the pieced FG unit from Step 25. *Fig. M*

27. Take one blue Small FG unit and one 2½in × 8½in neutral print rectangle. Join the rectangle to the left-hand short edge of the FG unit. *Fig. N*

Join this strip to the left-hand side of the pieced unit from Step 26.

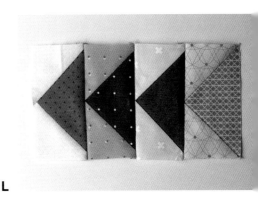

L

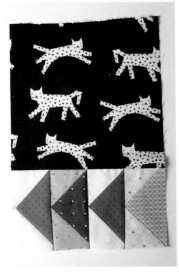

M

N

O

28. Take one 2½in × 12½in blue print rectangle. Sew it to the right-hand side of the unit from Step 27 to complete one blue Block B. *Fig. O*

29. Repeat Steps 25–28 to make a total of twenty-three of blue Block B.

30. Repeat Steps 25–28 using a pink 8½in square to complete one pink Block B.

Assembling the Quilt Top

31. Take the A and B blocks and arrange them into eight rows of six blocks each, matching up the black prints and alternating the blocks to create the arrow effect. Refer to the photo for fabric placement.

32. Join the blocks into rows, then join the rows to complete the quilt top.

Get creative with your block layout to get a good balance of prints across the quilt.

Quilting and Finishing

33. Cut the backing fabric in half across the width. Remove the selvedges and re-join the pieces with a ½in seam. Press the seam open.

34. Press the quilt top and backing well. Make a quilt sandwich by placing the backing fabric right side down, the batting on top, then the quilt top centrally and right side up. Baste the layers together using your preferred method.

35. Quilt as desired. Nicole quilted straight diagonal lines across the quilt.

36. Trim off the excess batting and backing fabric and square up the quilt.

37. Join the binding strips together end-to-end using diagonal seams. Press the seams open and trim away the dog-ears, then fold in half lengthwise, WST, and press.

38. Sew the binding to the front of the quilt, folding a mitre at each corner.

39. Fold the binding over to the back of the quilt and hand stitch it in place to finish.

Add a bold colour pop print to one of your arrow blocks.

Quilting with pink thread adds to the colour pop effect.

ABOUT THE CONTRIBUTORS

Check out these contributor websites for more great content! For additional resources, visit *Love Patchwork & Quilting* at lovepatchworkandquilting.com.

Jeni Baker (United States)

Gaggle of Geese (page 33) originally appeared in issue 3 of *Love Patchwork & Quilting*.

Website: incolororder.com

Instagram: @jenib320

Nicole Calver (Canada)

Desert Crossing (page 39), *Colour Twist* (page 60), *Space Blossom* (page 88), and *Looking Up* (page 103) originally appeared in issues 26, 40, 42, and 51 of *Love Patchwork & Quilting*.

Website: snipssnippets.ca

Instagram: @snipssnippets

Amanda Castor (United States)

Star Crossed (page 65) and *Heading South* (page 78) originally appeared in issues 47 and 13 of *Love Patchwork & Quilting*.

Website: materialgirlquilts.wordpress.com

Instagram: @materialgirlquilts

Elizabeth Dackson
(United States)

Rainbow Brights (page 82) originally appeared in issue 20 of *Love Patchwork & Quilting*.

Website: dontcallmebetsy.com

Instagram: @dontcallmebetsy

Moira de Carvalho (Australia)

Onward and Upward (page 50) originally appeared in issue 32 of *Love Patchwork & Quilting*.

Website: quiltdesignduo.com

Instagram: @quiltdesignduo

Jemima Flendt (Australia)

Folksy Flock (page 69) originally appeared in issue 48 of *Love Patchwork & Quilting*.

Website: tiedwitharibbon.com

Instagram: @tiedwitharibbon

Karen Lewis (England)

Colour Study 1 (page 15), *Sun Baked* (page 20), *Fancy Flora* (page 25), and *Colour Study 2* (page 29) originally appeared in issues 47, 49, 50, and 54 of *Love Patchwork & Quilting*.

Website: karenlewistextiles.com

Instagram: @karenlewistextiles

Jenn Nevitt (United States)

Light and Dark (page 11) originally appeared in issue 44 of *Love Patchwork & Quilting*.

Instagram: @mommysew

Peta Peace (Australia)

Pastel Twist (page 6) and *Summer Scoop* (page 54) originally appeared in issues 39 and 36 of *Love Patchwork & Quilting*.

Website: shequiltsalot.com

Instagram: @shequiltsalot

Minki Kim (United States)

Dear Diary (page 74) originally appeared in issue 59 of *Love Patchwork & Quilting*.

Website: minkikim.com

Instagram: @zeriano

Julie Rutter (Scotland)

All Around Arrows (page 95) originally appeared in issue 48 of *Love Patchwork & Quilting*.

Website: blackisleyarns.co.uk

Instagram: @blackisleyarns

Want even more creative content?

Make it, snap it, share it *using* *#ctpublishing*